PIANO • VOCAL • GUITAR

CHRIST IS RISEN!
26 EASTER SONGS CELEBRATING THE RESURRECTION

ISBN 978-1-4584-1697-1

HAL•LEONARD®
CORPORATION
7777 W. BLUEMOUND RD. P.O. BOX 13819 MILWAUKEE, WI 53213

Visit Hal Leonard Online at
www.halleonard.com

ALIVE FOREVER AMEN

Words and Music by TRAVIS COTTRELL,
SUE C. SMITH and DAVID MOFFITT

With excitement

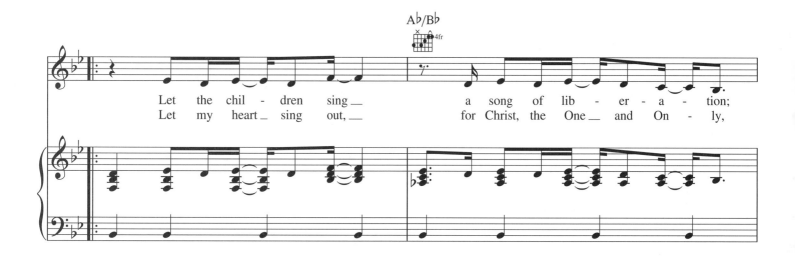

Let the chil-dren sing ___ a song of lib-er-a-tion;

Let my heart ___ sing out, ___ for Christ, the One ___ and On- ly,

the God of our ___ sal-va-tion set us ___ free. ___

so pow-er-ful ___ and ho- ly, res-cued ___ me. ___

Death, where is ___ thy sting? ___ The curse of sin ___ is bro - ken.
Death won't hurt ___ me now, ___ be-cause He has ___ re - deemed ___ me.

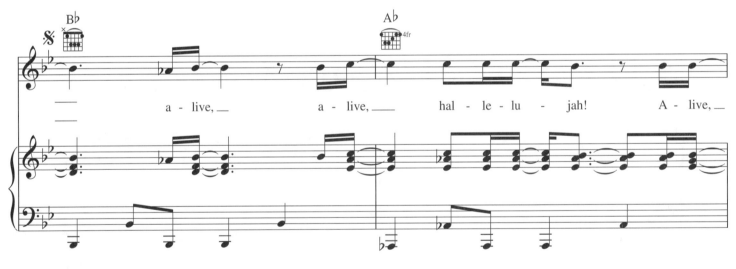

The emp - ty tomb ___ stands o - pen; come and ___ see. ___ He's a - live, ___
No grave will ev - er keep ___ me from my ___ King. ___ A - live, ___

___ a - live, ___ a - live, ___ hal - le - lu - jah! A - live, ___

___ praise and glo - ry to ___ the Lamb. ___ A - live, ___

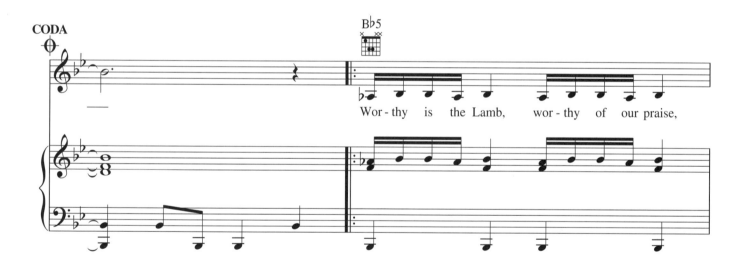

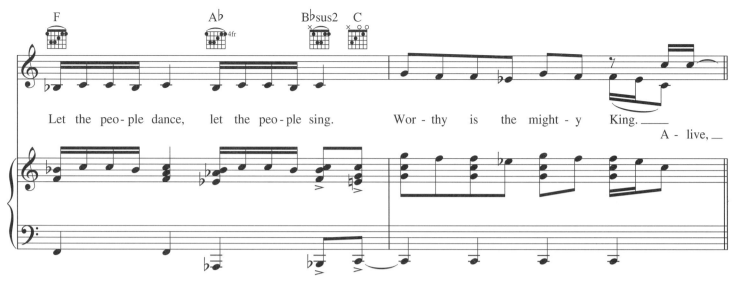

Let the peo-ple dance, let the peo-ple sing. Wor-thy is the might-y King. ___ A - live, ___

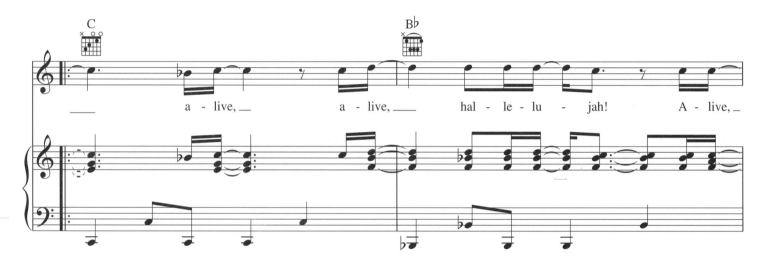

___ a - live, ___ a - live, ___ hal - le - lu - jah! A - live, ___

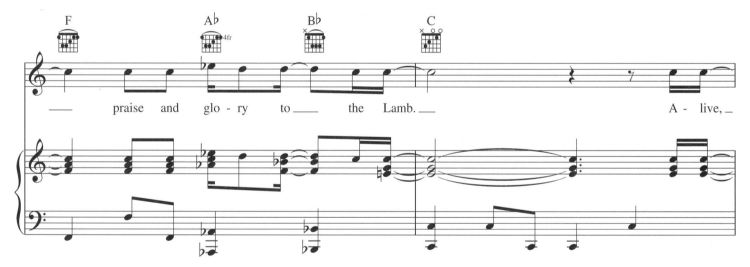

___ praise and glo - ry to ___ the Lamb. ___ A - live, ___

___ a - live, ___ a - live, ___ hal - le - lu - jah! A - live ___

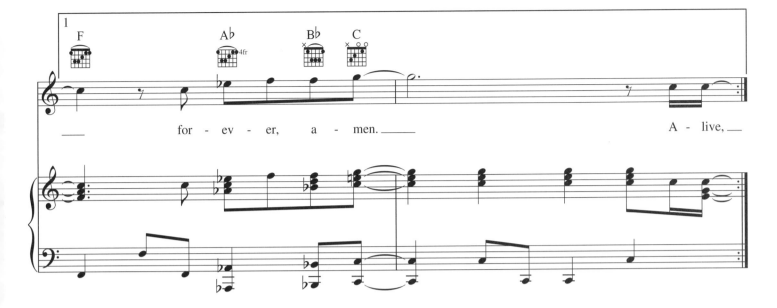

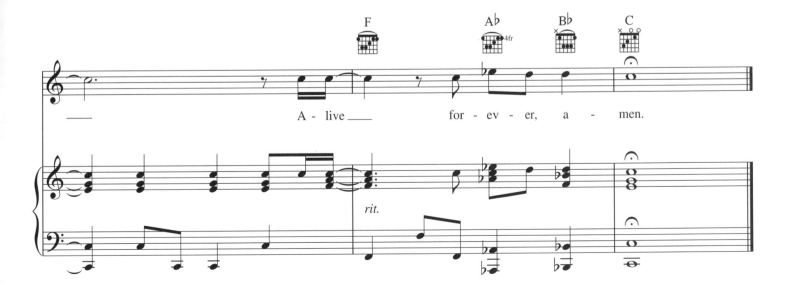

ALIVE IN US

Words and Music by JASON INGRAM
and REUBEN MORGAN

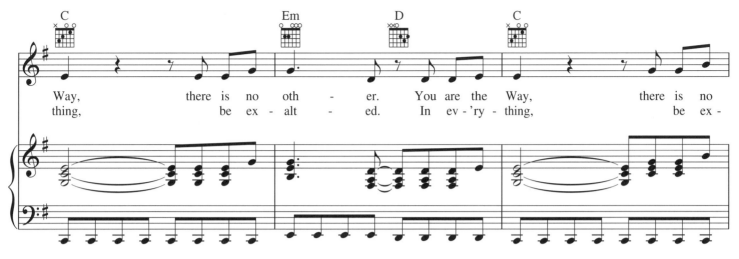

Way, there is no oth - er. You are the Way, there is no
thing, be ex - alt - ed. In ev - 'ry - thing, be ex -

oth - er. You rose from death to vic - to - ry. You
alt - ed. reign in life,

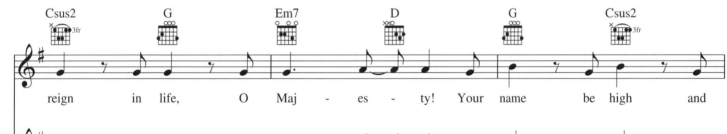

reign in life, O Maj - es - ty! Your name be high and

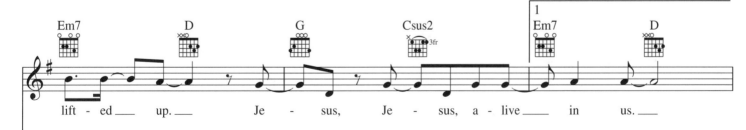

lift - ed up. Je - sus, Je - sus, a - live in us.

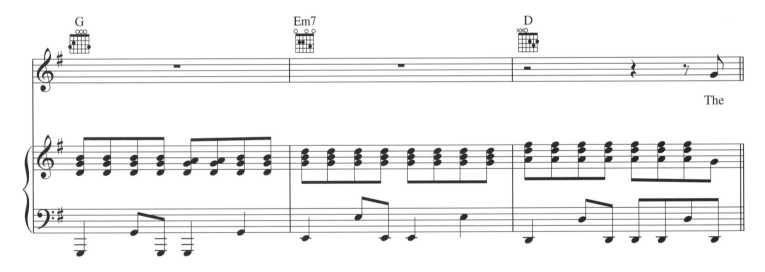

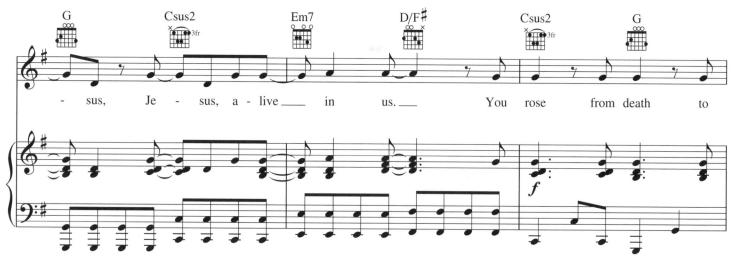

-sus, Je - sus, a - live___ in us.___ You rose from death to

vic - to - ry.___ You reign in life, O Maj - es - ty! Your

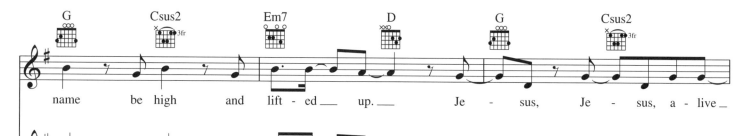

name be high and lift - ed___ up.___ Je - sus, Je - sus, a - live___

___ in us.___ Je - sus, Je - sus, a - live___ in us.___

ALL THE EARTH WILL SING YOUR PRAISES

Words and Music by
PAUL BALOCHE

Driving beat

You lived, You died, You said in

three days You would rise. You did, You're a - live.

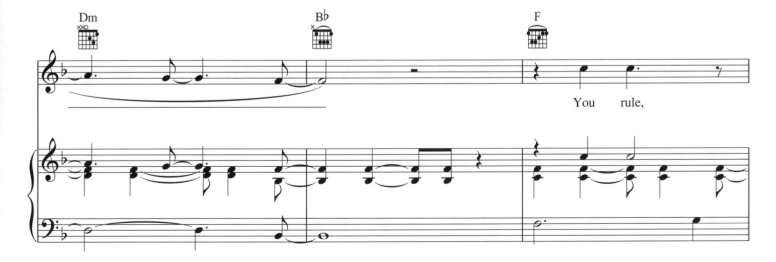

You rule,

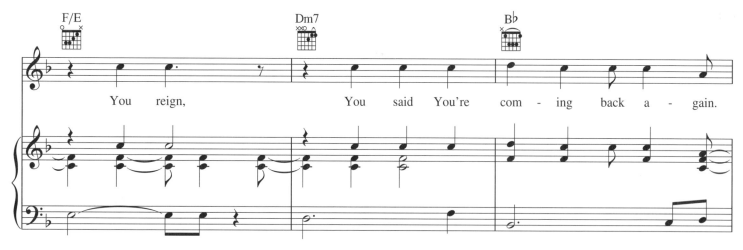

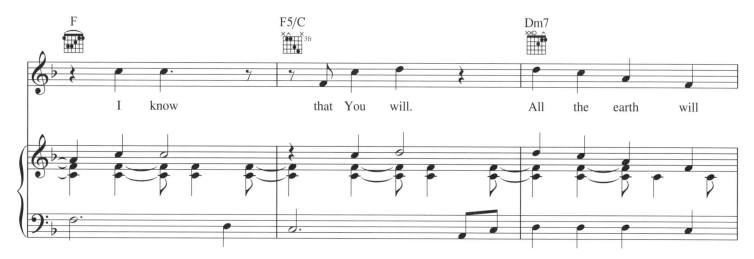

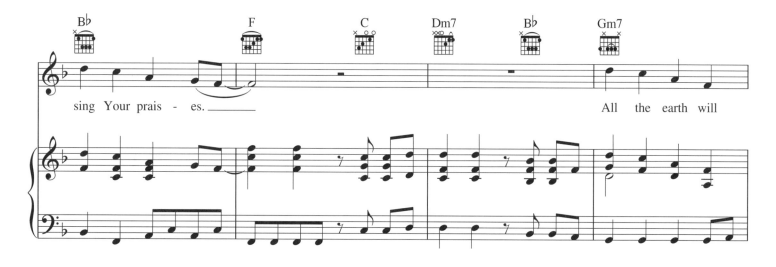

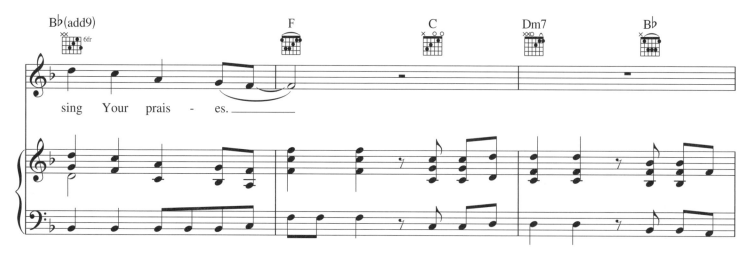

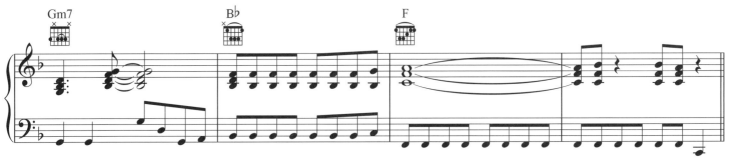

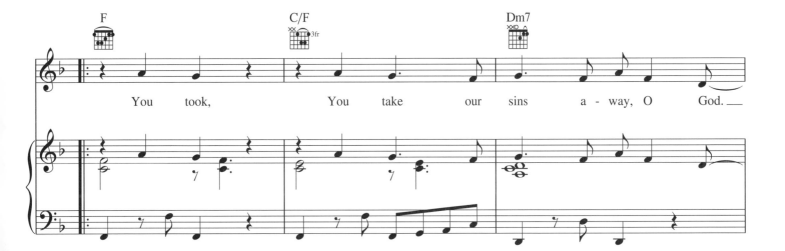

You took,   You take   our sins   a - way, O   God. ___

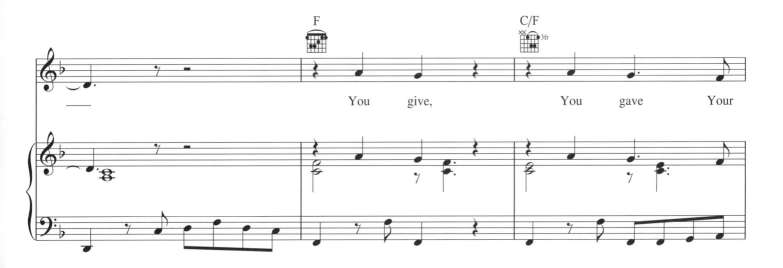

___   You give,   You gave   Your

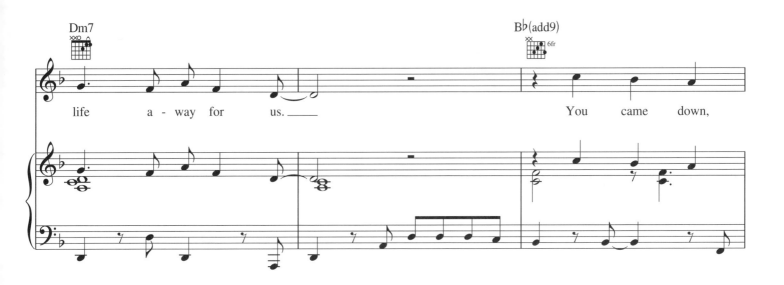

life a - way for   us. ___   You came down,

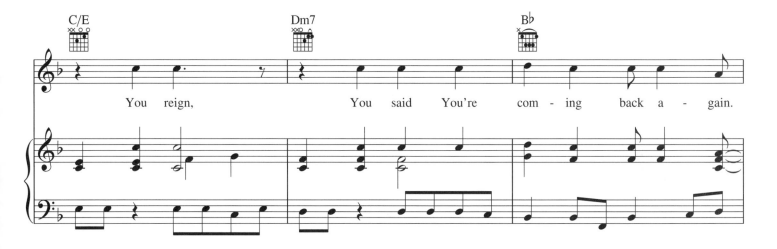

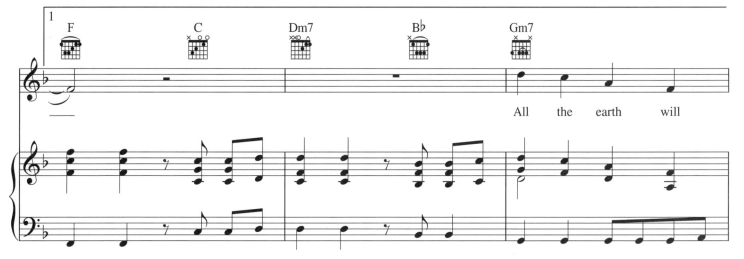

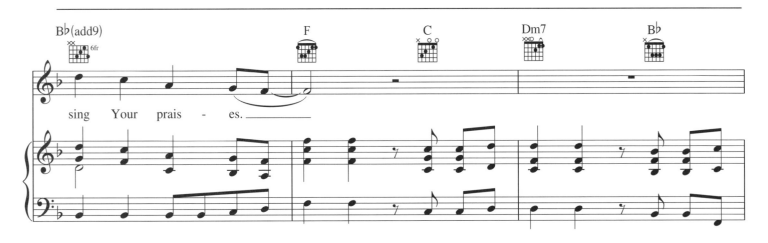

sing Your prais - es. _____

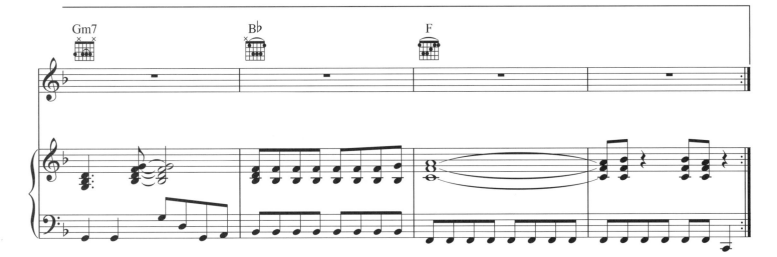

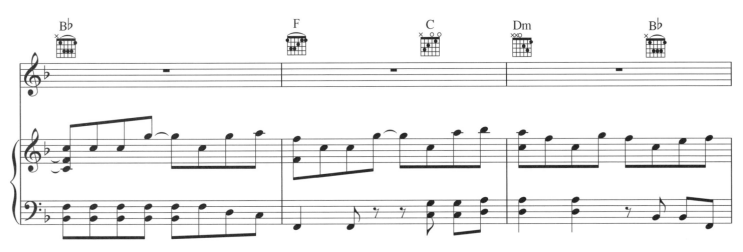

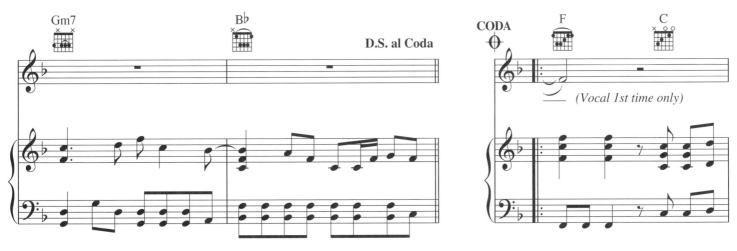

D.S. al Coda

CODA

(Vocal 1st time only)

All the earth will sing Your prais - es. ____

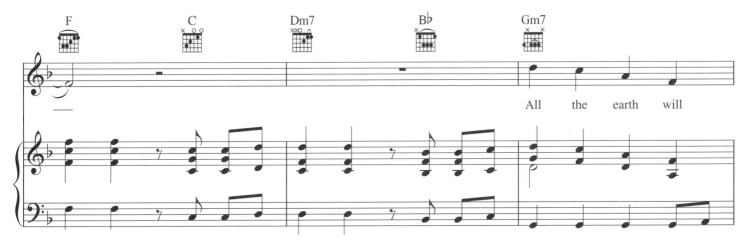

____ All the earth will

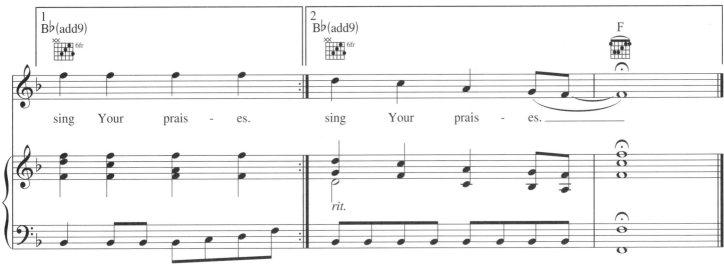

sing Your prais - es.

sing Your prais - es. ____

rit.

ARISE, MY LOVE

Words and Music by
EDDIE CARSWELL

Slowly, mysteriously

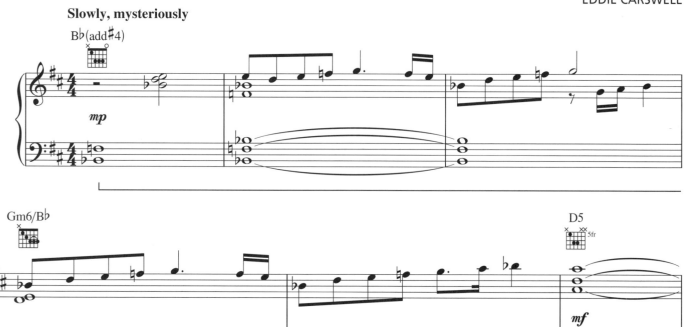

Not a word was heard at the tomb that day, just

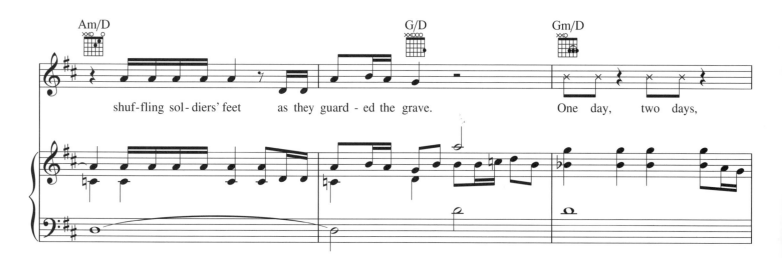

shuf-fling sol-diers' feet as they guard-ed the grave. One day, two days,

my Love, _ a - rise, _ my Love. _ The grave _ no _ long- er has a hold _

_ on _ You. No more _ death's sting, no more suf - fer - ing. A -

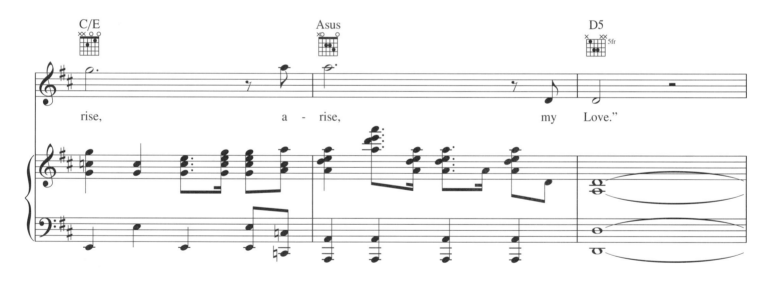

rise, a - rise, my Love."

The earth trem - bled and the tomb be - gan to shake,

and like light-ning from heav-en the stone rolled _ a - way. And as dead men, the guards

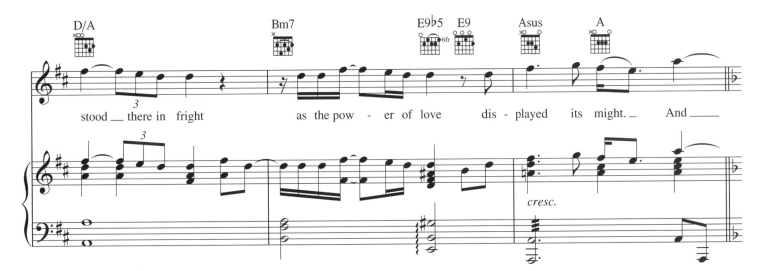

stood _ there in fright as the pow - er of love dis - played its might. _ And _

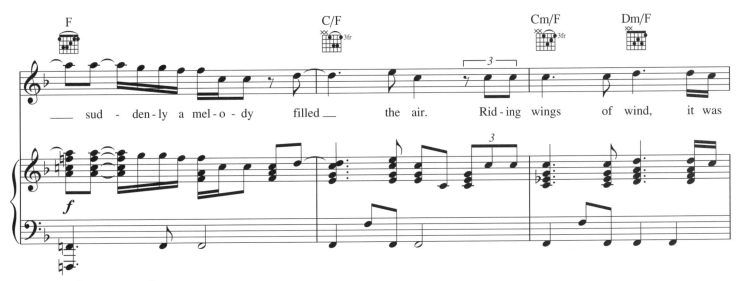

_ sud - den-ly a mel-o-dy filled _ the air. Rid-ing wings of wind, it was

ev - 'ry - where. _ The words all cre-a-tion had been long - ing to hear, _ a

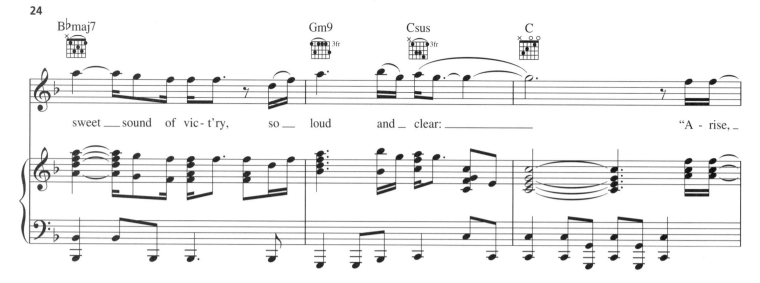

sweet ___ sound of vic - t'ry, so ___ loud and ___ clear: _____ "A - rise, ___

___ my Love, ___ a - rise, ___ my Love. ___ The grave ___ no ___ long - er has a hold ___

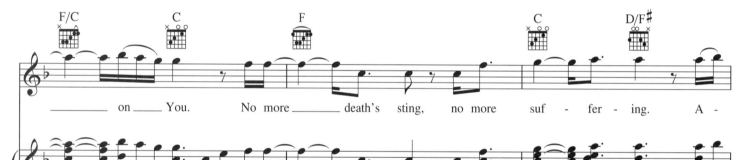

_____ on ___ You. No more _____ death's sting, no more suf - fer - ing. A -

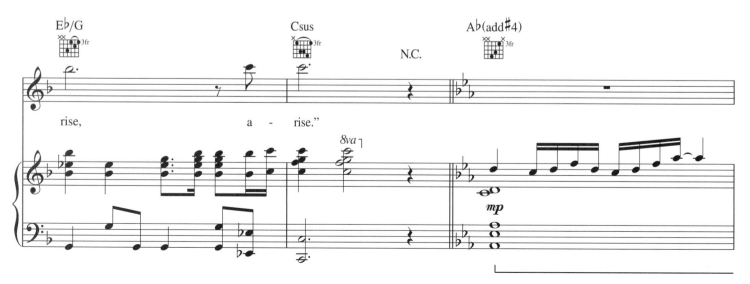

rise, ___ a - rise."

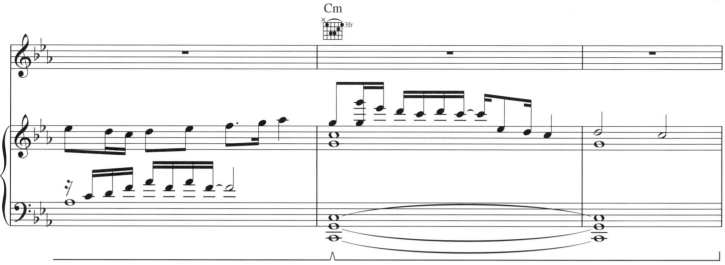

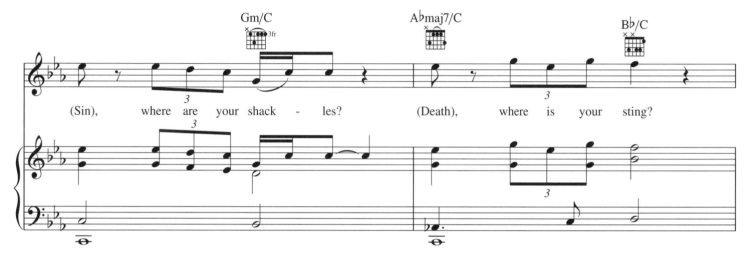

(Sin), where are your shack - les? (Death), where is your sting?

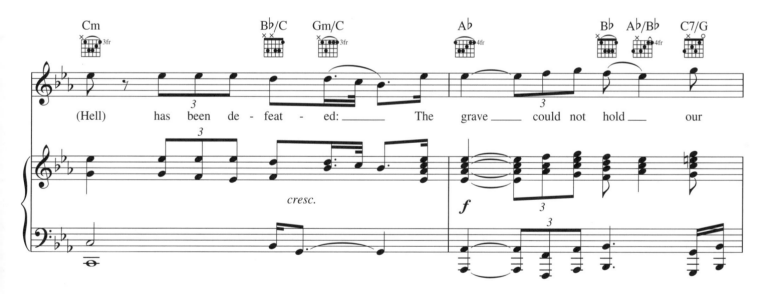

(Hell) has been de - feat - ed: _____ The grave _____ could not hold _____ our

cresc.

_f_

King.

"A - rise, __

my Love, ___ a - rise, ___ my Love. ___ The grave ___

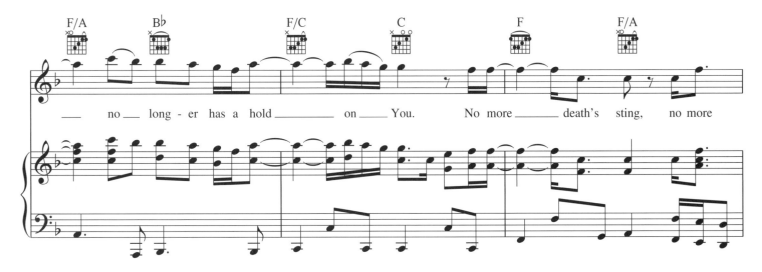

___ no ___ long - er has a hold ___ on ___ You. No more ___ death's sting, no more

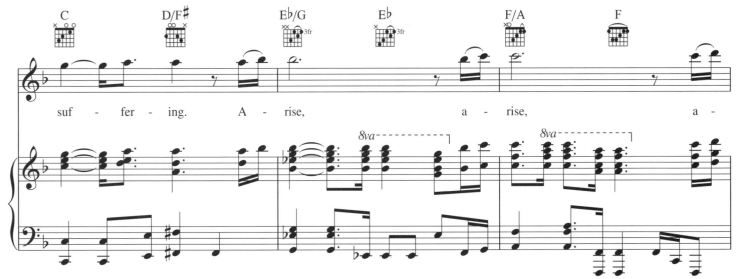

suf - fer - ing. A - rise, ___ a - rise, ___ a -

rise!"

BECAUSE HE LIVES

Words by WILLIAM J. and GLORIA GAITHER
Music by WILLIAM J. GAITHER

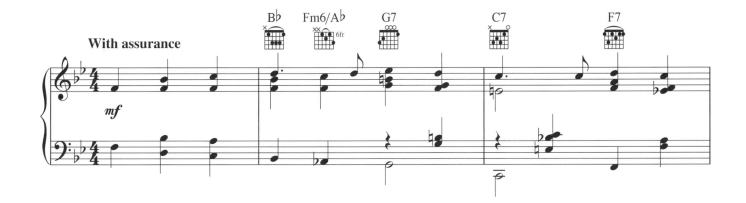

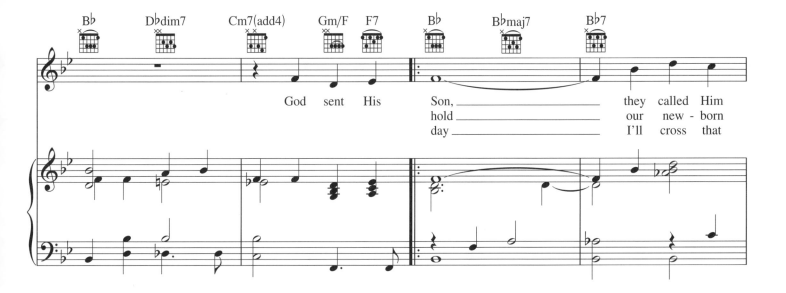

God sent His Son, ____ they called Him
hold ____ our new-born
day ____ I'll cross that

Je - sus; He came to love, ____ heal and for-
ba - by, and feel the pride ____ and joy he
riv - er; I'll fight life's fi - nal war with

CELEBRATE JESUS

Words and Music by
GARY OLIVER

Driving

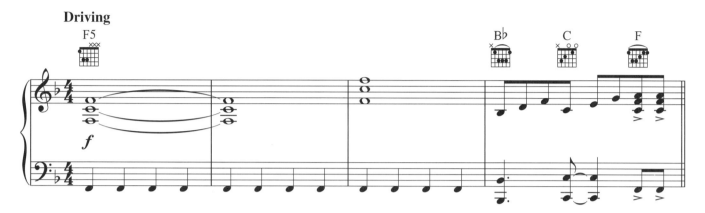

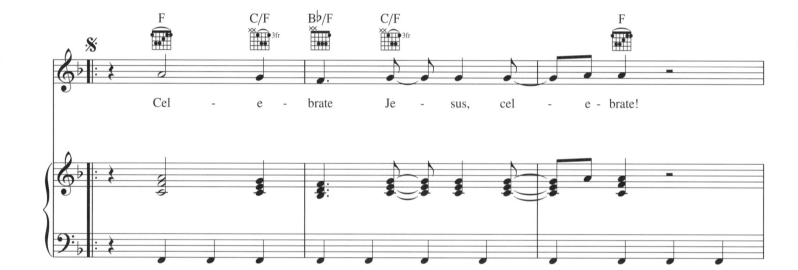

Cel - e - brate Je - sus, cel - e - brate!

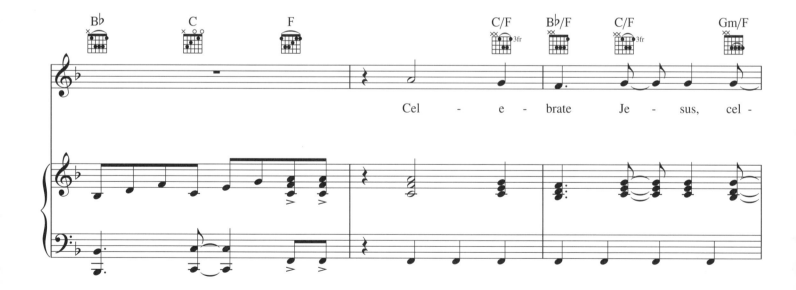

Cel - e - brate Je - sus, cel -

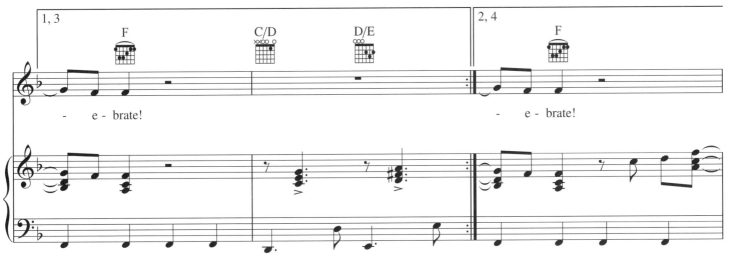

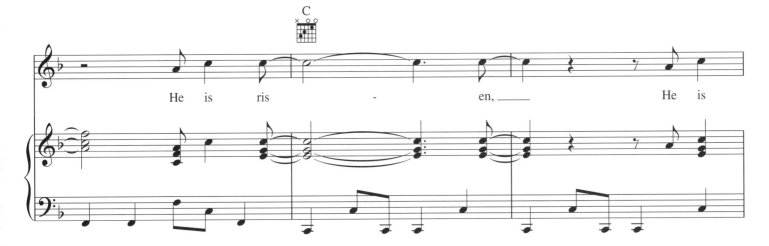

FOR ALL YOU'VE DONE

Words and Music by
REUBEN MORGAN

Up-tempo Rock

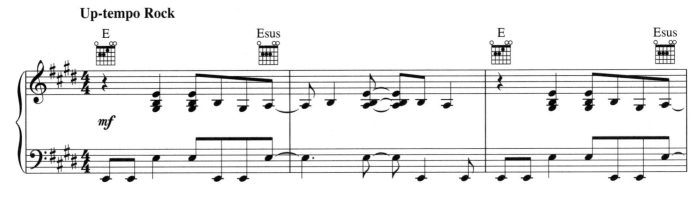

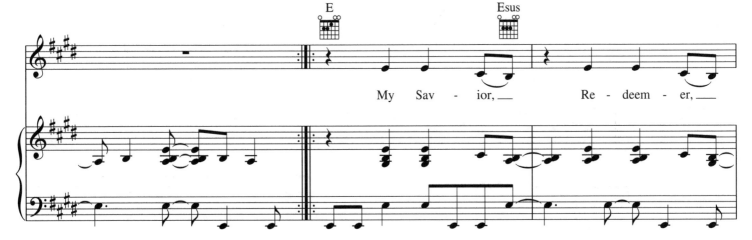

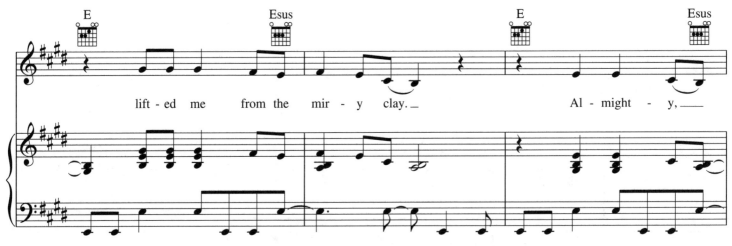

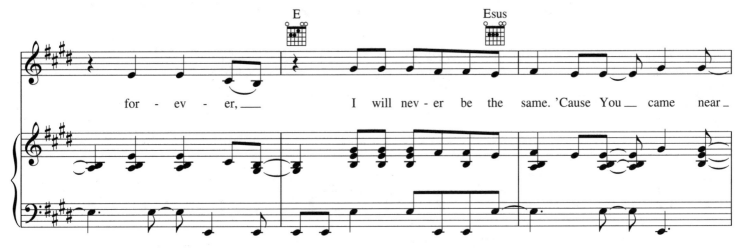

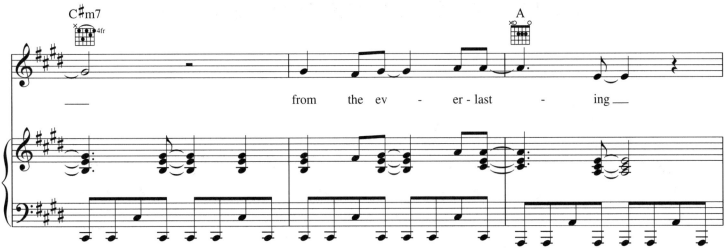

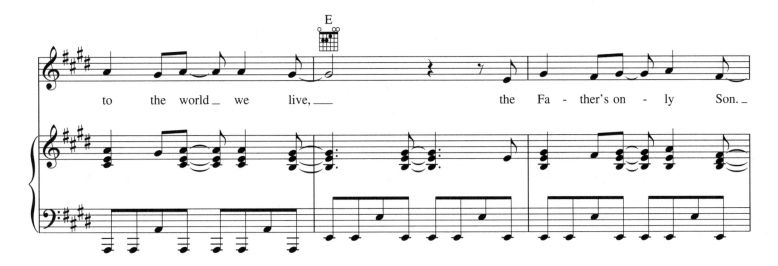

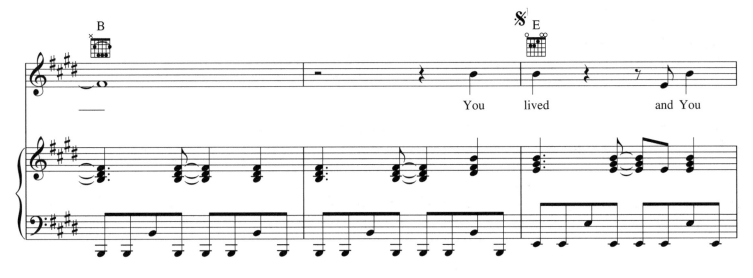

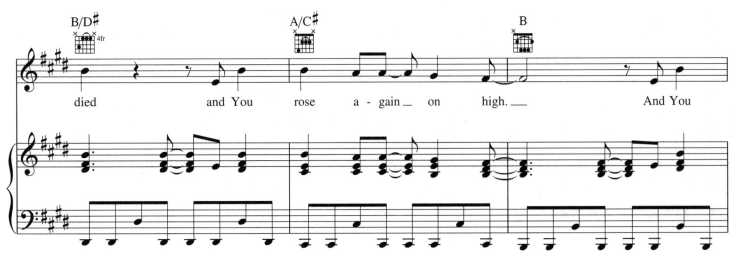

o - pened _ the way ___ for the world ___ to live ___ a - gain. ___

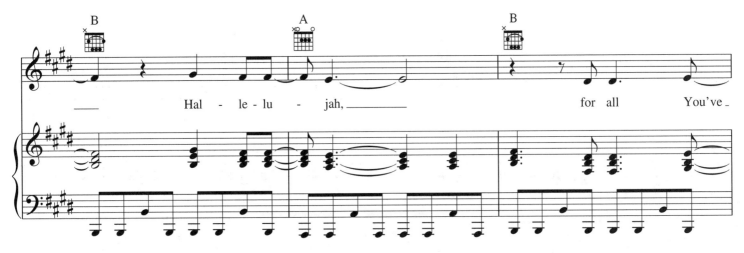

___ Hal - le - lu - jah, _____ for all You've_

___ done. _____

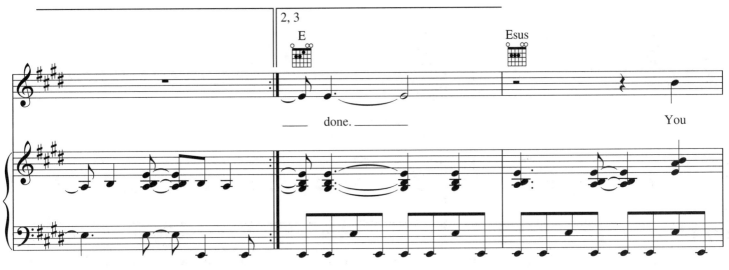

___ done. _____ You

lived   and You died   and You rose a - gain __ on high. __

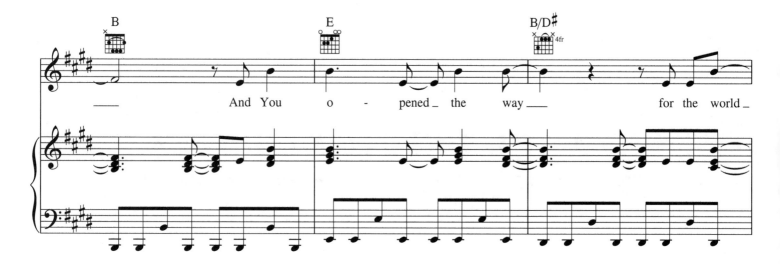

__ And You o - pened __ the way __   for the world __

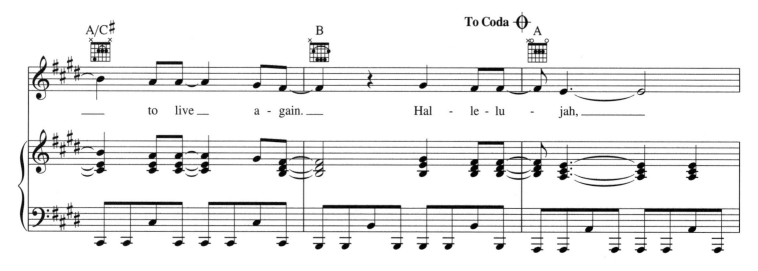

__ to live __ a - gain. __ Hal - le - lu - jah, _____

for all You've __ done. _____
(Vocal 1st time only)

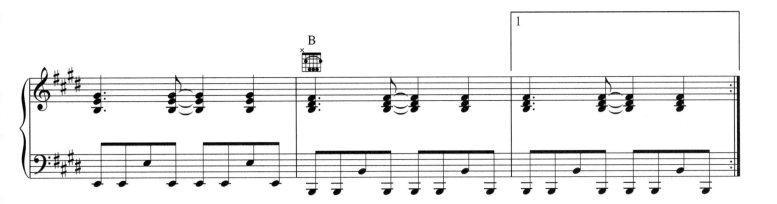

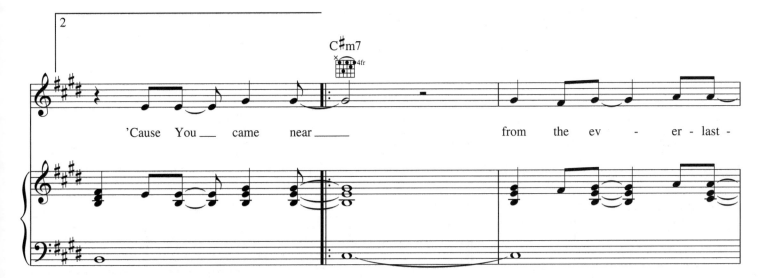

'Cause You ___ came near ___ from the ev - er - last -

- ing ___ to the world ___ we live, ___ the

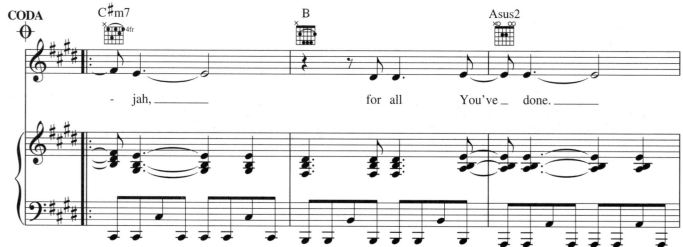

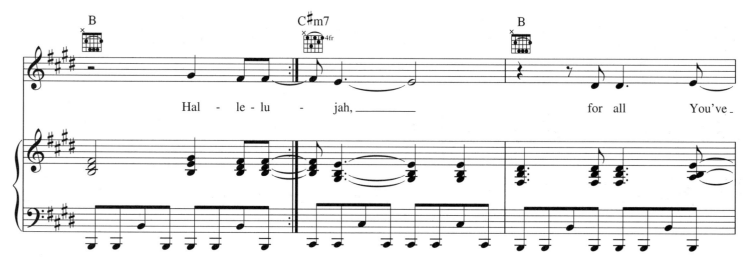

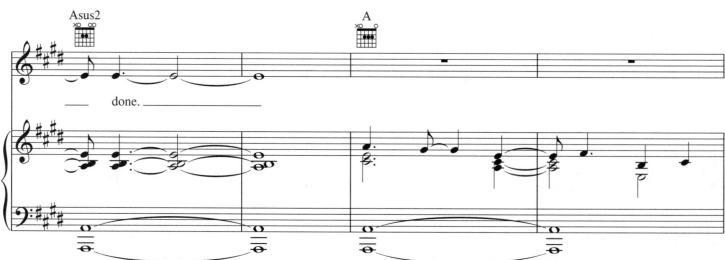

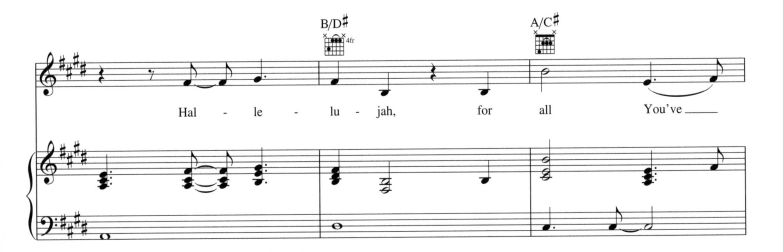

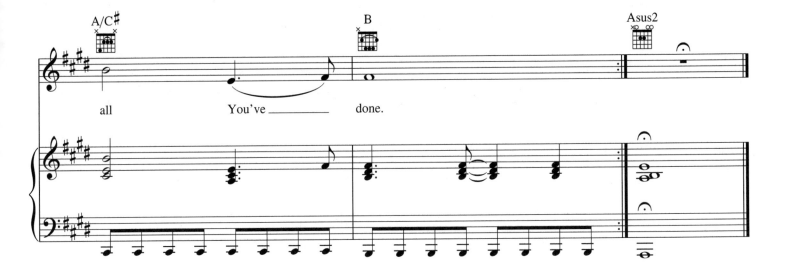

CHRIST IS RISEN

Words and Music by MIA FIELDES
and MATT MAHER

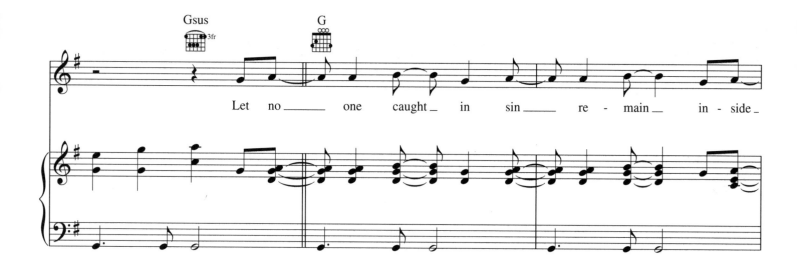

* Recorded a half step lower.

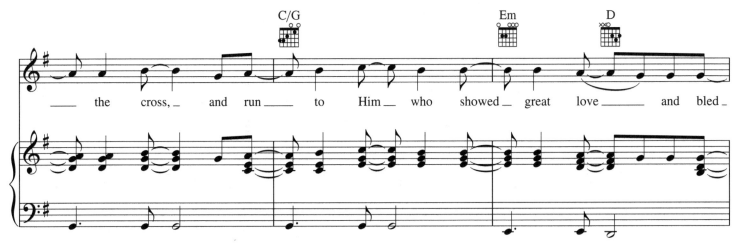

the cross, and run to Him who showed great love and bled

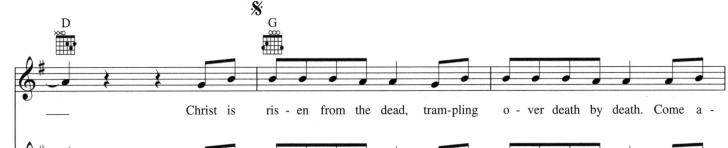

for us. Free-ly You've bled for us.

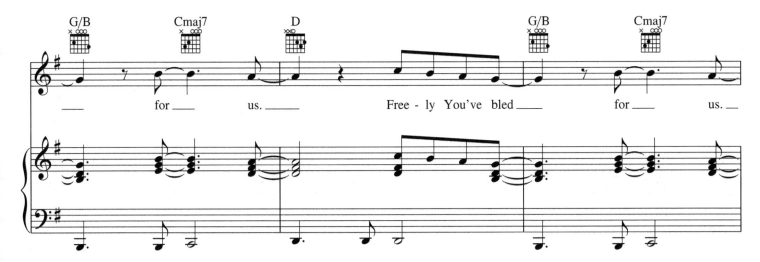

Christ is ris-en from the dead, tram-pling o-ver death by death. Come a-

wake, come a-wake, come and rise up from the grave. Christ is ris-en from the dead; we are

one with Him a-gain. Come a-wake, come a-wake, come and rise up from the grave. ___

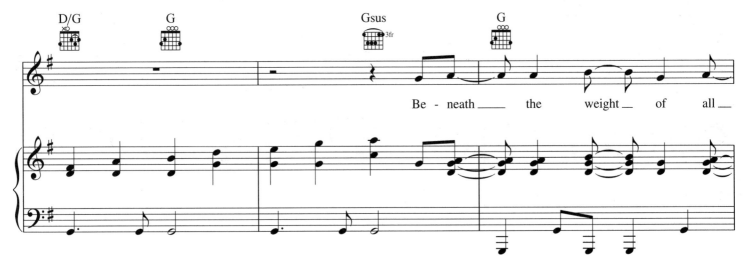

Be - neath ___ the weight ___ of all ___

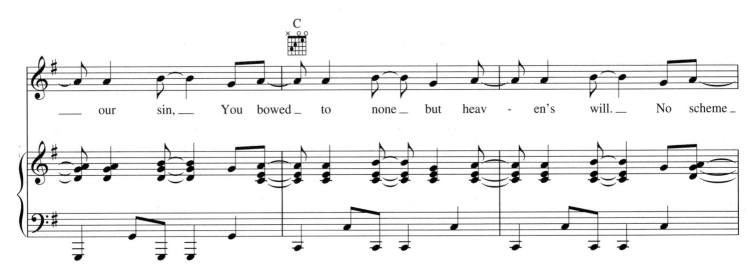

___ our sin, ___ You bowed ___ to none ___ but heav - en's will. ___ No scheme ___

___ of hell, ___ no scof - fer's crown, ___ no bur - den great ___ can hold ___

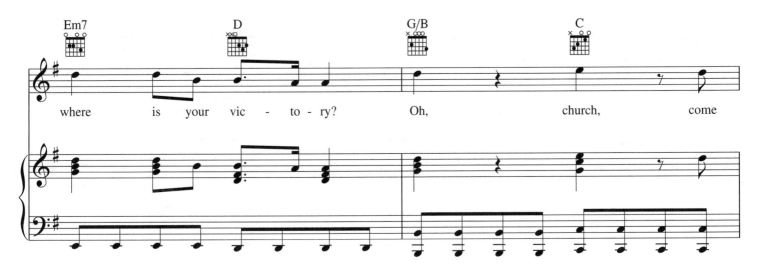

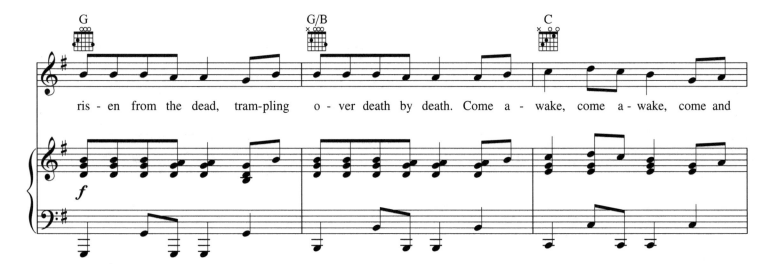

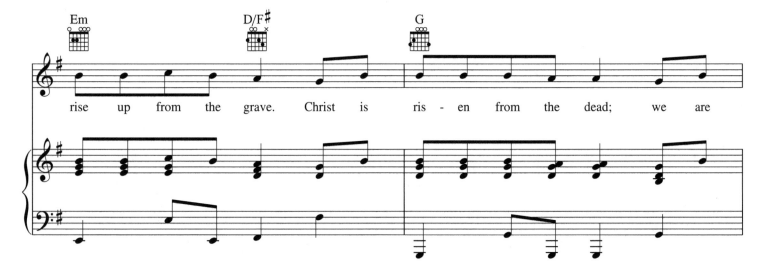

ris-en from the dead, tram-pling o - ver death by death. Come a - wake, come a - wake, come and

rise up from the grave. Christ is ris - en from the dead; we are one with Him a - gain. Come a -

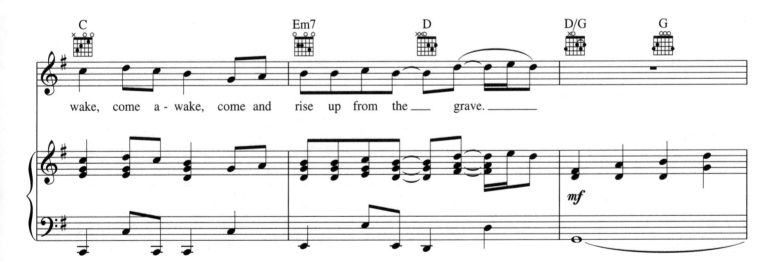

wake, come a - wake, come and rise up from the ___ grave. ___

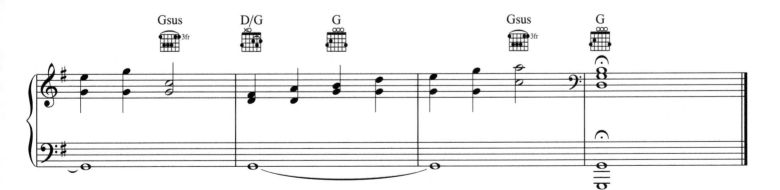

EASTER SONG

Words and Music by
ANNE HERRING

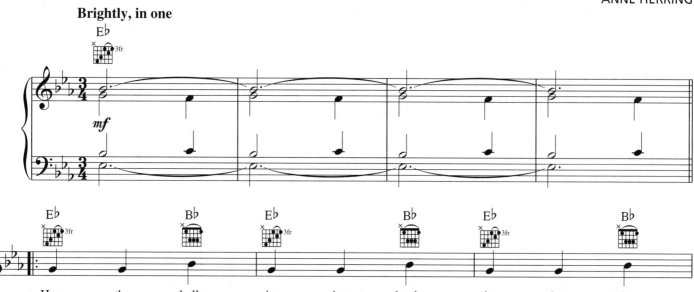

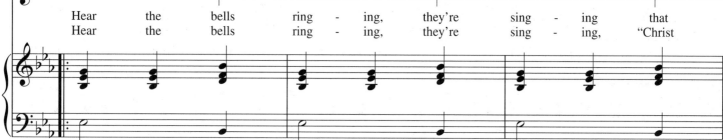

Hear the bells ring - ing, they're sing - ing that
Hear the bells ring - ing, they're sing - ing, "Christ

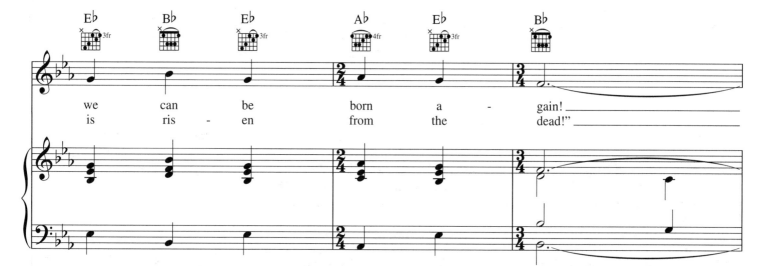

we can be born a - gain! _____
is ris - en from the dead!" _____

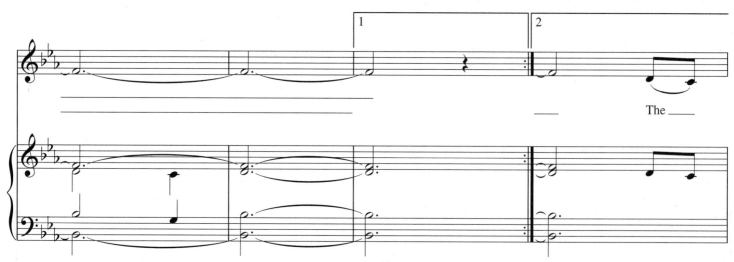

The ___

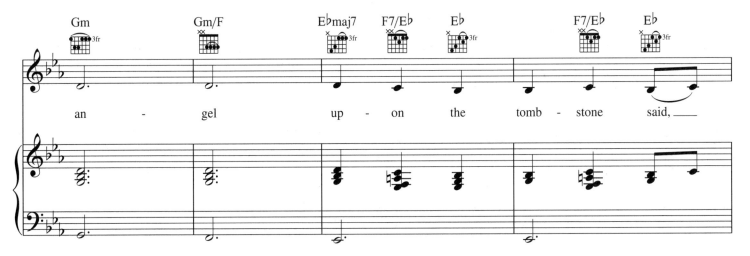

an - gel up - on the tomb - stone said, ____

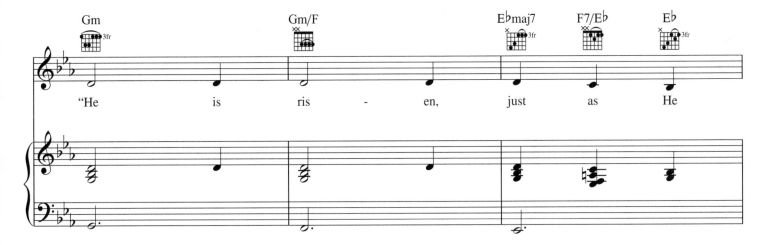

"He is ris - en, just as He

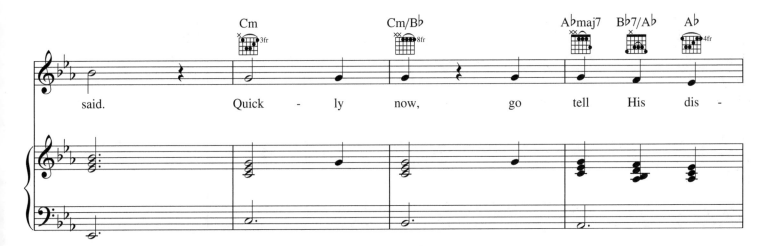

said. Quick - ly now, go tell His dis -

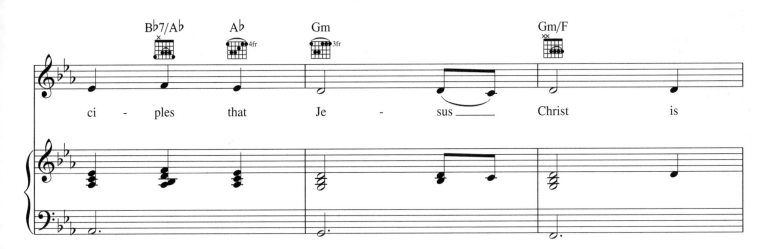

ci - ples that Je - sus ____ Christ is

no long - er dead!" _____ Joy

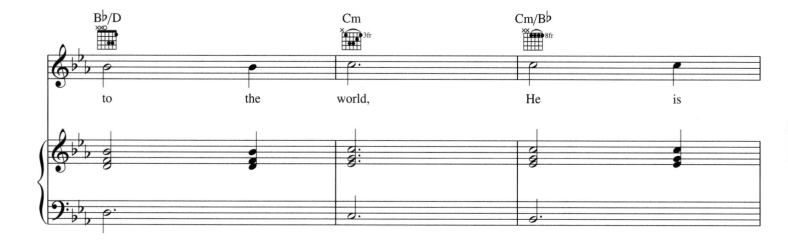

to the world, He is

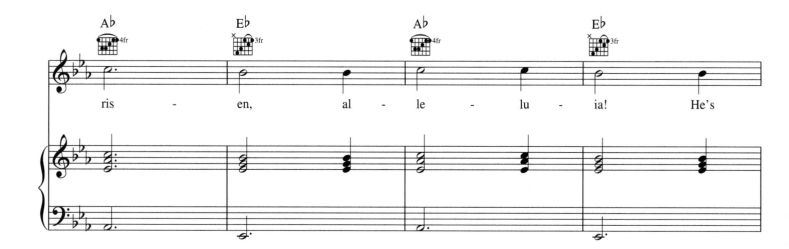

ris - en, al - le - lu - ia! He's

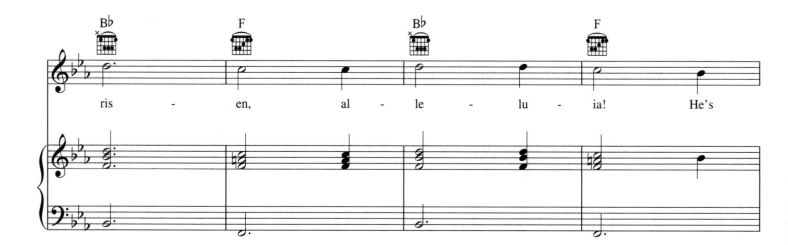

ris - en, al - le - lu - ia! He's

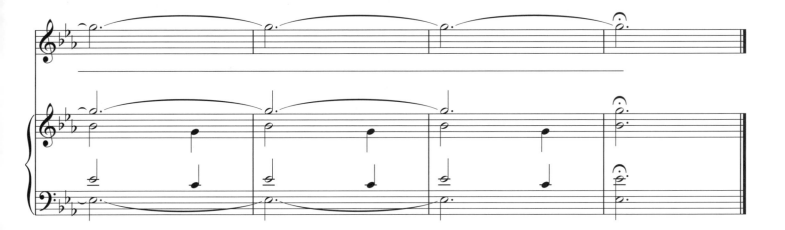

GLORIOUS

Words and Music by PAUL BALOCHE
and BRENTON BROWN

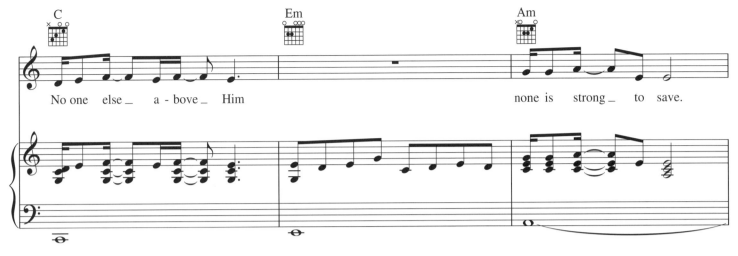

No one else _ a - bove _ Him   none is strong _ to save.

He a - lone _ has con - quered   the

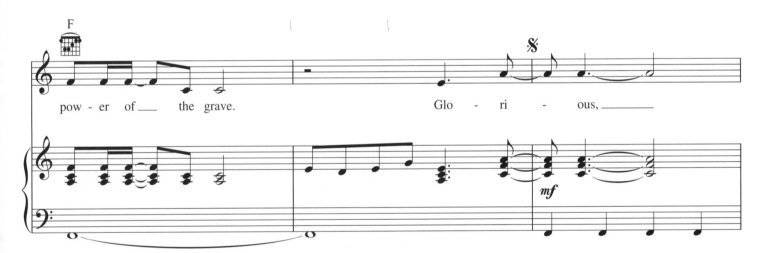

pow - er of __ the grave.   Glo - ri - ous, _____

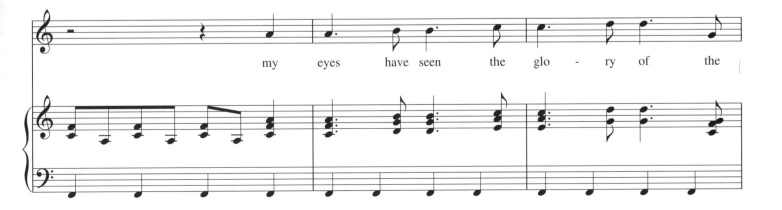

my eyes have seen the glo - ry of the

Lord.

Glo - ri - ous, _____

He stands a - bove the rul - ers of the

earth.

To Coda ⊕

Look be - yond __ the tomb - stone,

see the liv - ing God.

See the res - ur - rect - ed Rul - er of my heart.

No one else _ a - bove _ Him,

none to match _ His worth. The hope of His _ re - turn - ing

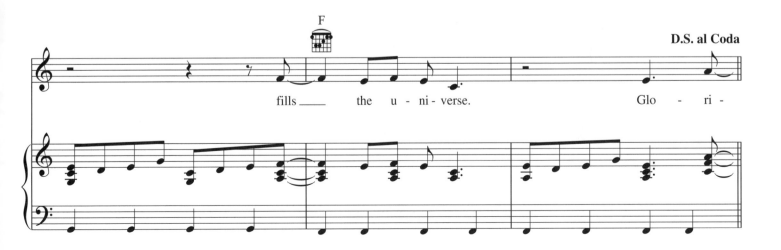

D.S. al Coda

fills _____ the u - ni - verse. Glo - ri -

CODA

Glo - ri - ous, _____ glo - ri -

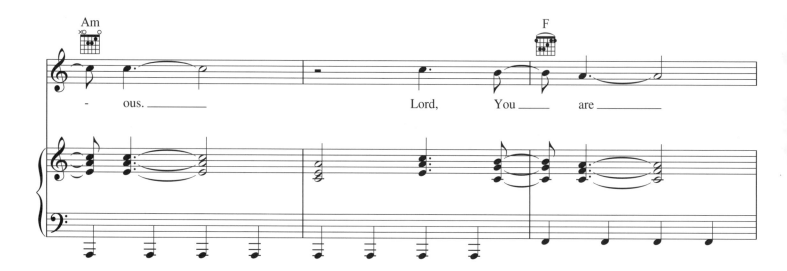

- ous. _____ Lord, You _____ are _____

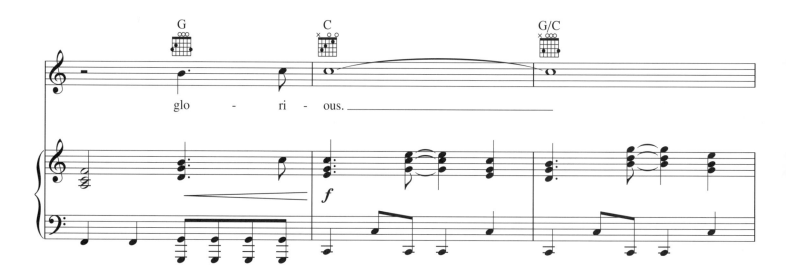

glo - ri - ous. _____

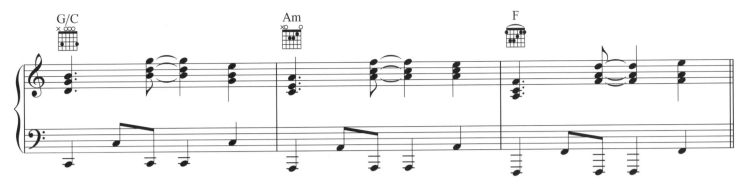

Oh, _____ oh, _____ oh. You are glo-

-ri - ous.   -ri - ous.   Glo - ri -

- ous, _____   my eyes have seen the

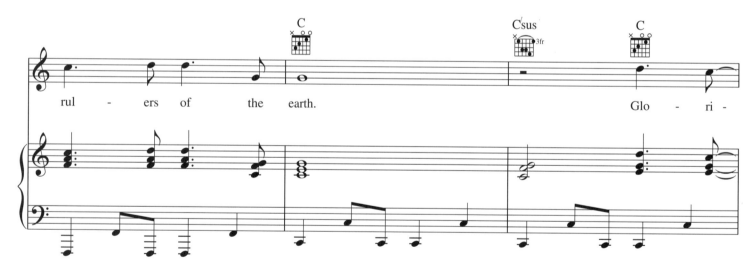

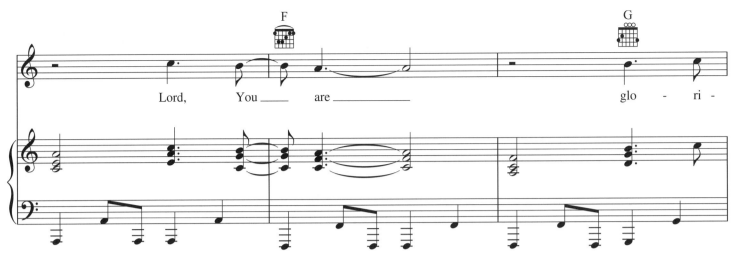

Lord, You ___ are ___ glo - ri -

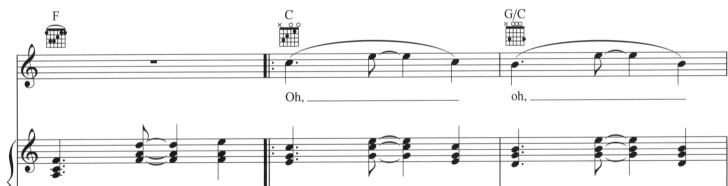

ous. ___

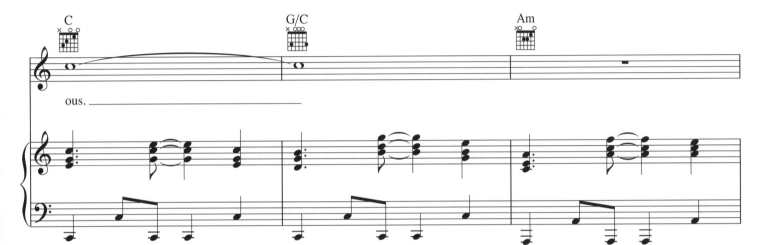

Oh, ___ oh, ___

oh. You are glo - ri - ous. ___ - ri - ous.

GLORIOUS DAY
(Living He Loved Me)

Words and Music by MARK HALL
and MICHAEL BLEAKER

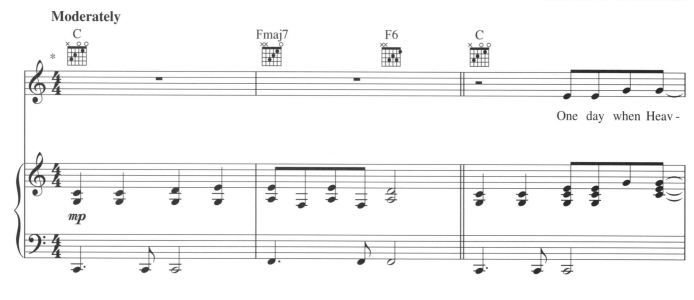

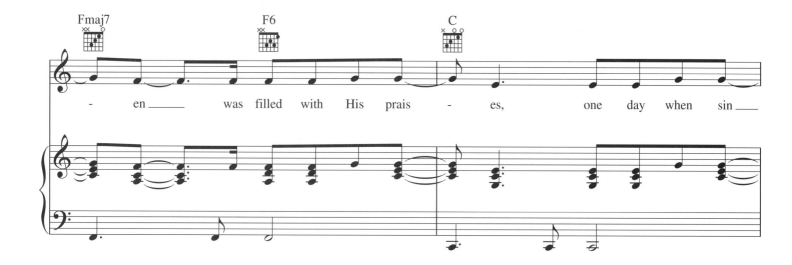

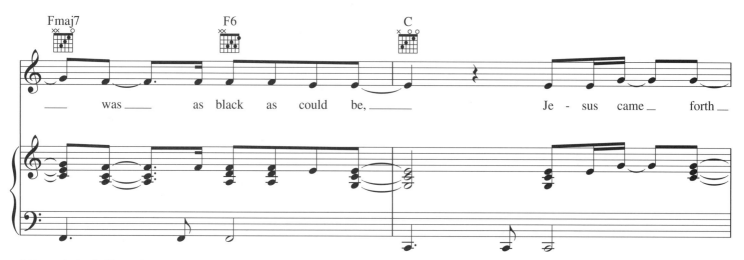

Recorded a half step lower.

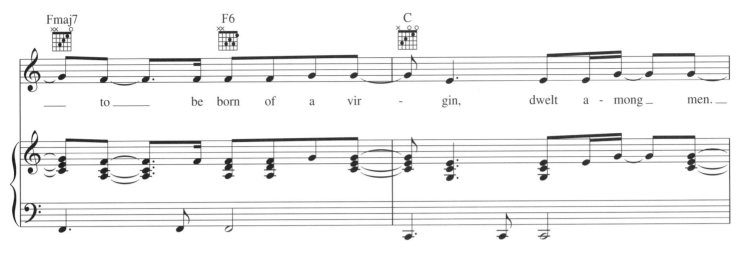

to be born of a vir - gin, dwelt a - mong men.

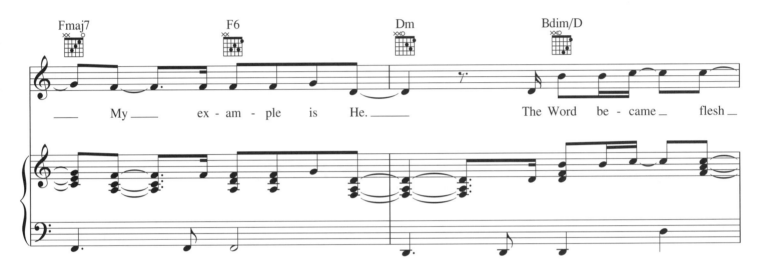

My ex - am - ple is He. The Word be - came flesh

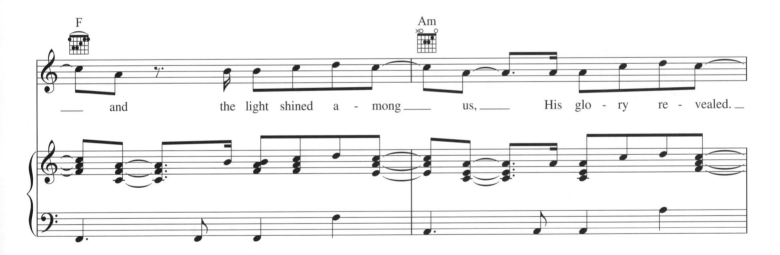

and the light shined a - mong us, His glo - ry re - vealed.

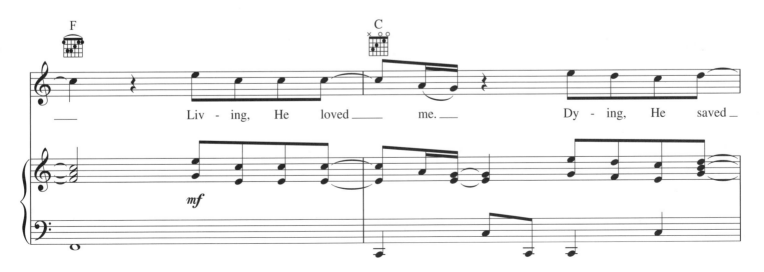

Liv - ing, He loved me. Dy - ing, He saved

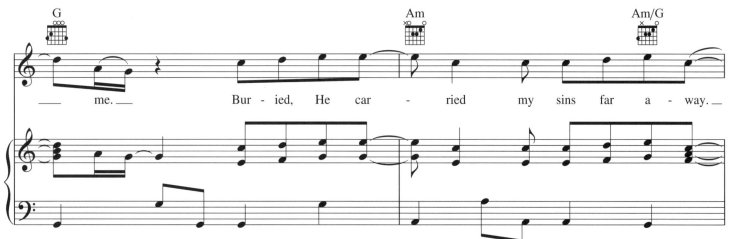

me. Bur - ied, He car - ried my sins far a - way.

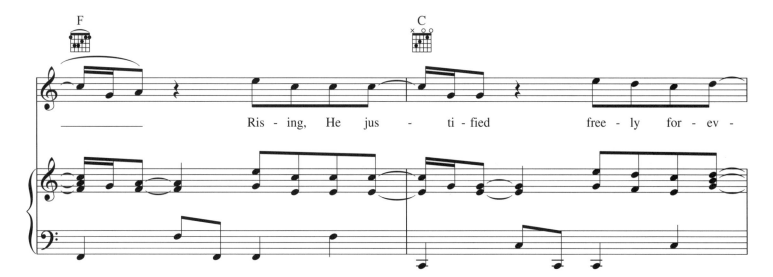

Ris - ing, He jus - ti - fied free - ly for - ev -

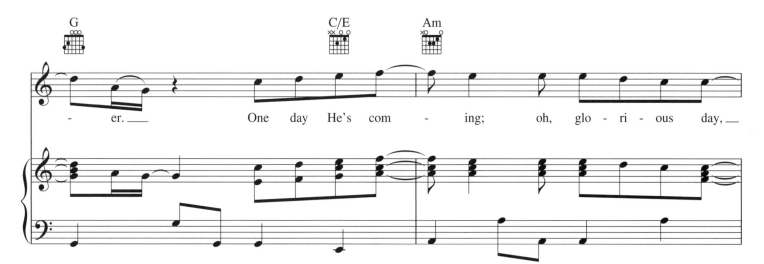

- er. One day He's com - ing; oh, glo - ri - ous day,

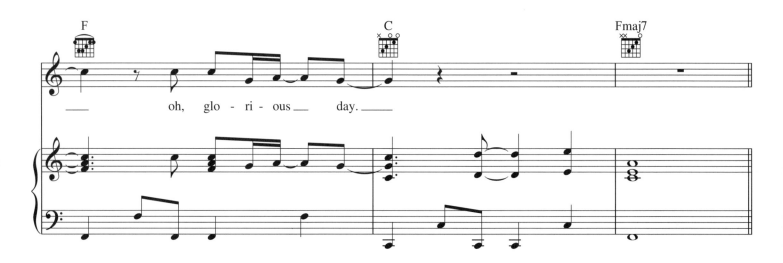

oh, glo - ri - ous day.

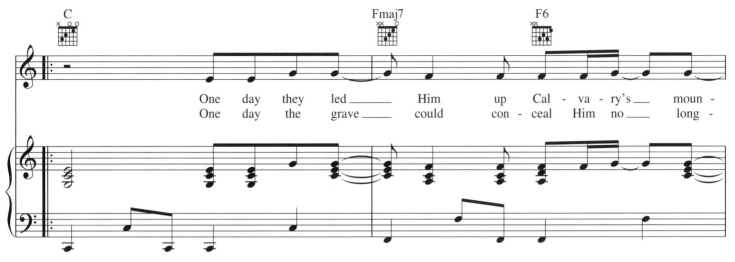

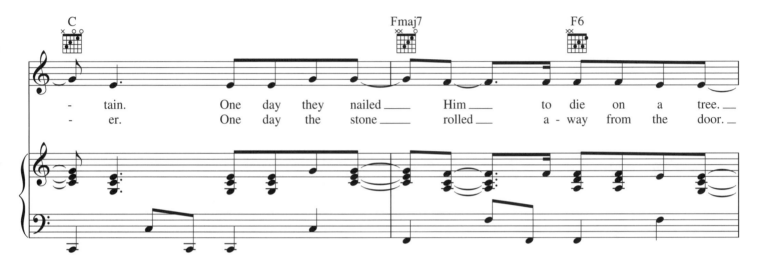

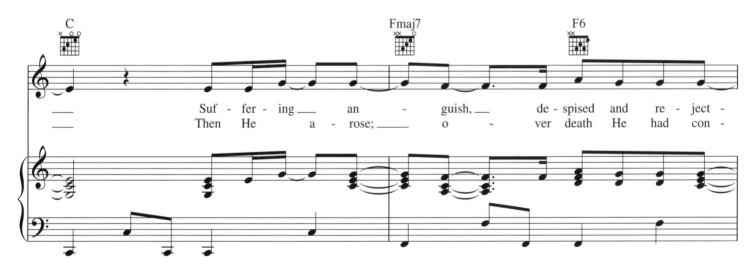

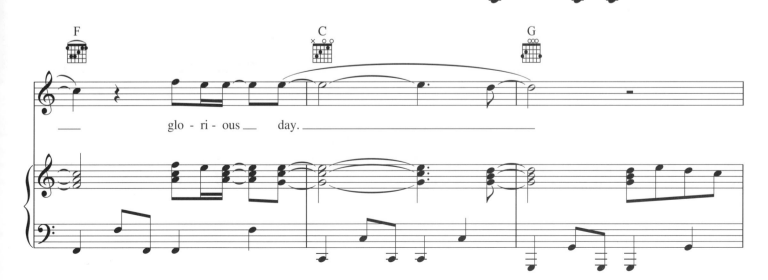

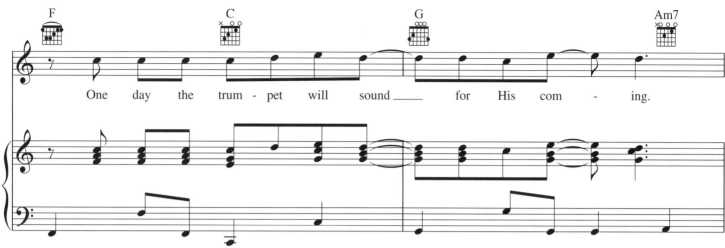

One day the trum - pet will sound ____ for His com - ing.

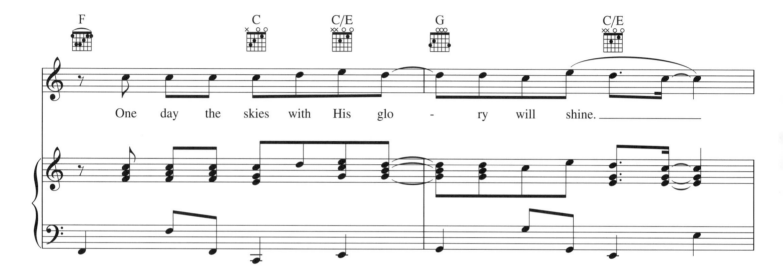

One day the skies with His glo - ry will shine. ____

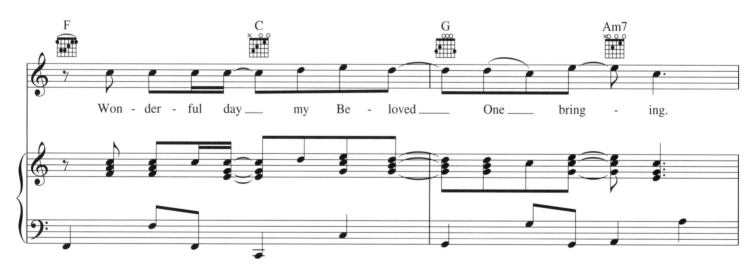

Won - der - ful day ____ my Be - loved ____ One ____ bring - ing.

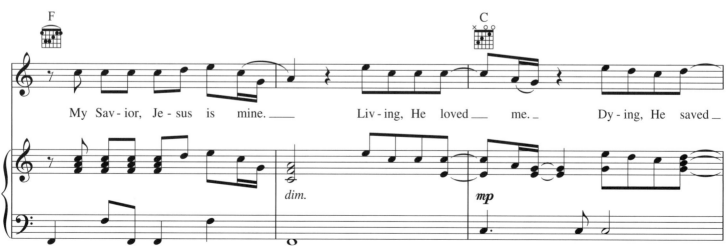

My Sav - ior, Je - sus is mine. ____ Liv - ing, He loved ____ me. _ Dy - ing, He saved _

dim.

mp

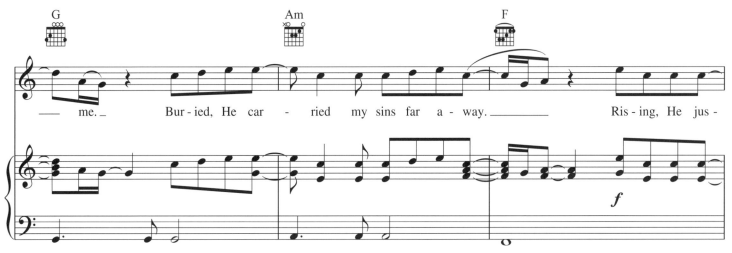

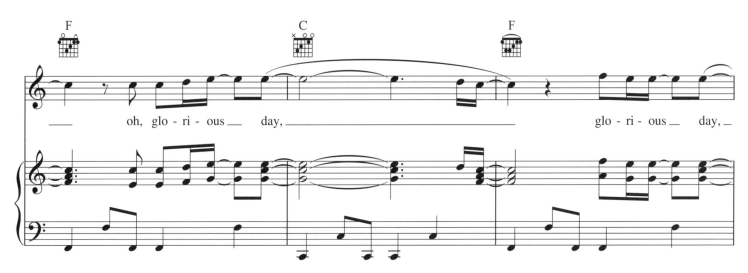

GOD'S NOT DEAD
(Like a Lion)

Words and Music by
DANIEL BASHTA

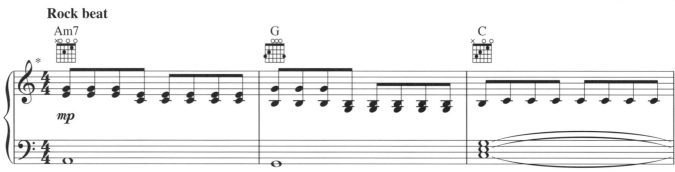

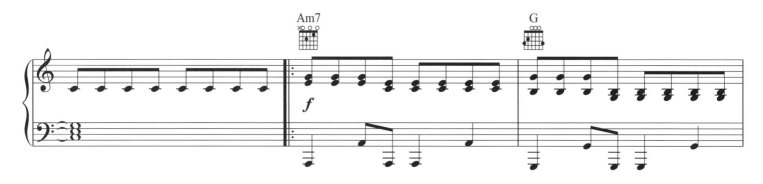

Recorded a half step lower.

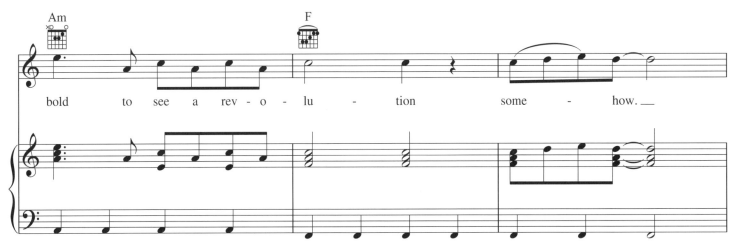

bold   to   see   a   rev - o - lu - tion   some - how. __

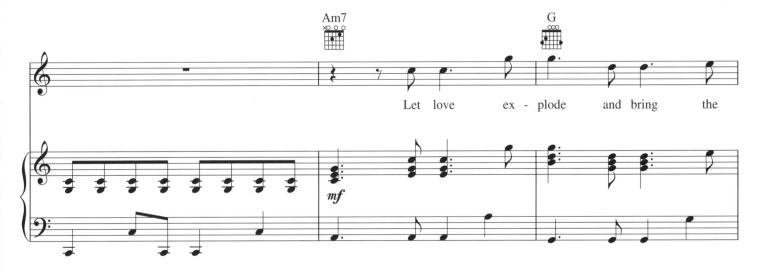

Let   love   ex - plode   and   bring   the

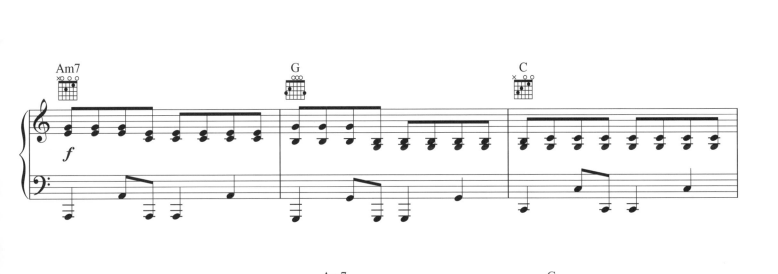

dead   to   life, _____

a   love   so   bold   to   bring   a   rev - o -

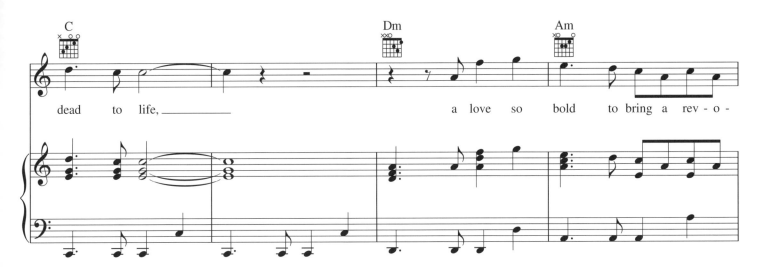

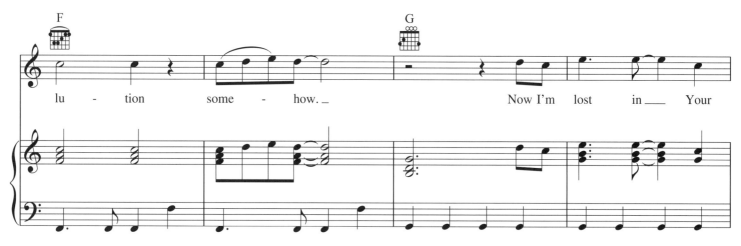

lu - tion some - how. _____ Now I'm lost in ___ Your

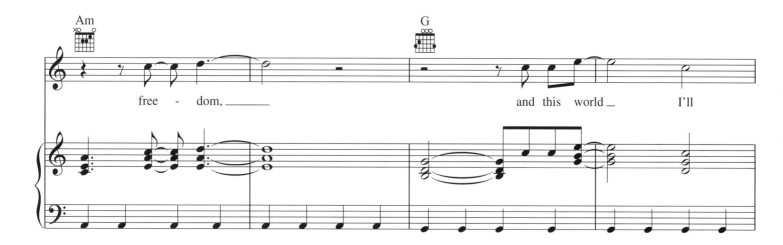

free - dom, _____ and this world __ I'll

o - ver - come. _____ My God's __ not dead; He's sure - ly a - live. __ He's liv-

-ing on the in - side, roar - ing like a li - on. God's not dead; He's

sure - ly a - live.__ He's liv - ing on the in - side, roar - ing like a li - on. Roar-

- ing, He's roar - ing, He's roar - ing like a li - on.__

Let hope a - rise and make the dark - ness hide._____

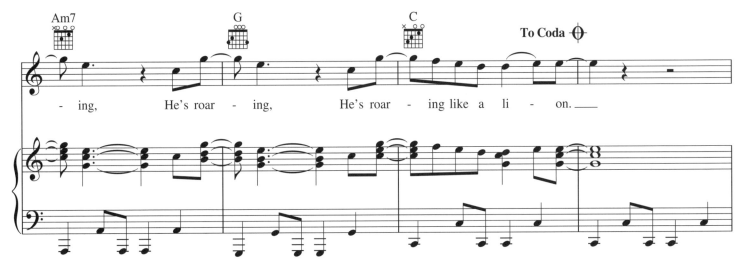

My faith is dead; I need a res - ur - rec - tion some - how.__

Now I'm lost in ___ Your free - dom, ___

and this world ___ I'll o - ver -

come. ___ My God's ___ not dead; He's sure - ly a - live. ___ He's liv -

He's roar - ing, He's roar - ing. Let Heav - en

roar and fi - re fall. Come shake the

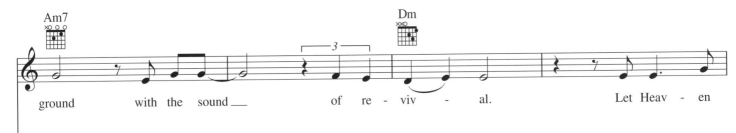

ground with the sound __ of re - viv - al. Let Heav - en

roar and fi - re fall.

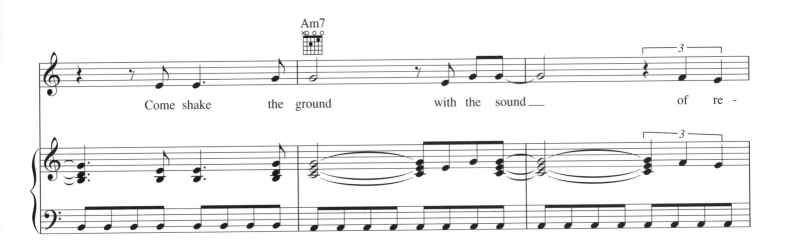

Come shake the ground with the sound __ of re -

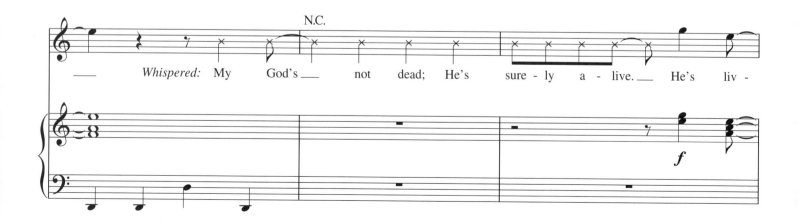

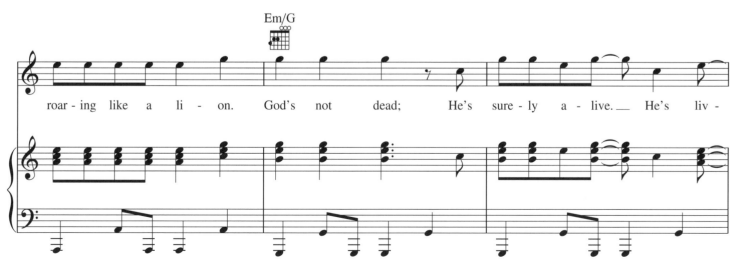

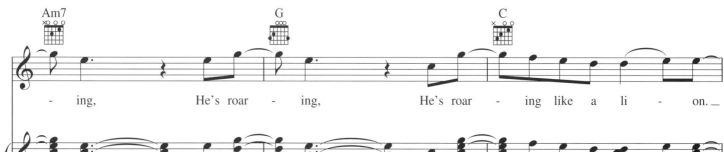

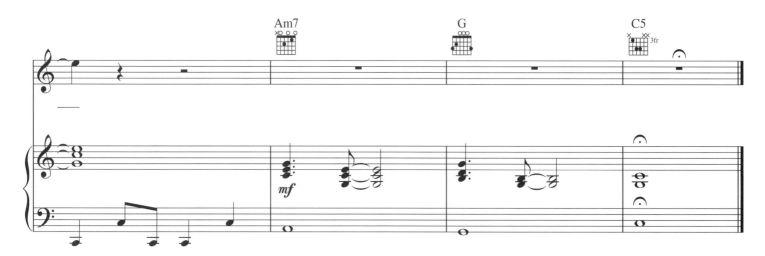

GOD IS ALIVE

Words and Music by STEVE FEE
and EDDIE KIRKLAND

Driving Rock beat

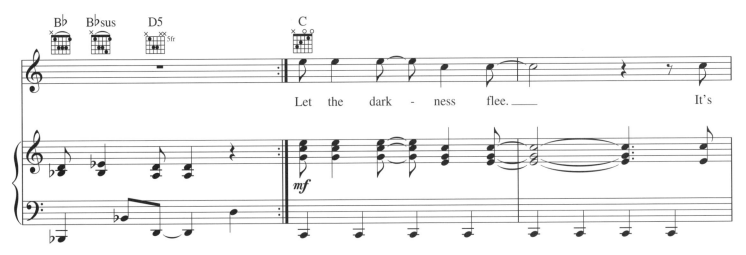

Let the dark-ness flee.___ It's

got no pow- er o- ver me. I___ have been___ set free.___

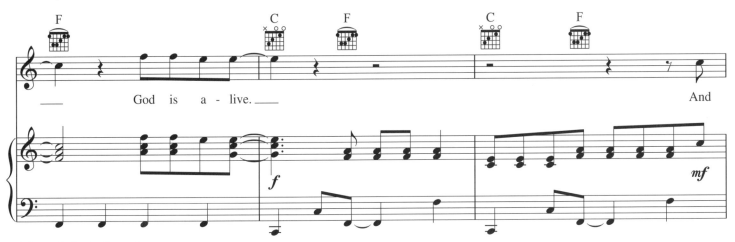

___ God is a- live.___ And

* Recorded a half step lower.

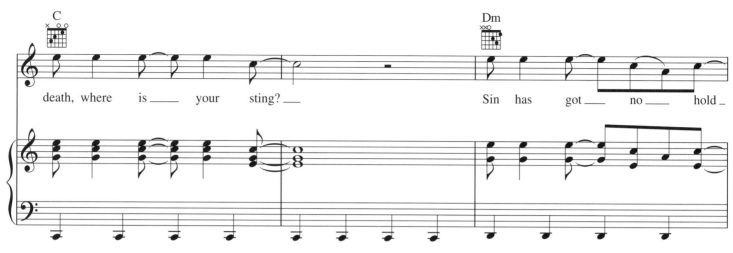

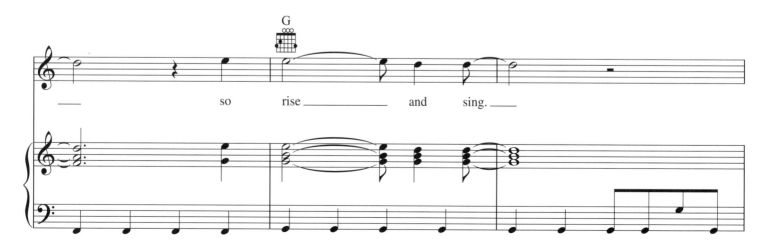

Ev - 'ry - one, glo - ri - fy the ris - en Son. The

Ho - ly One has o - ver - come. Je - sus is a -

live. The en - e - my is

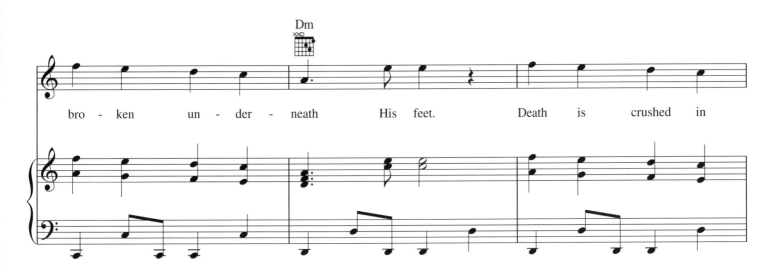

bro - ken un - der - neath His feet. Death is crushed in

vic - to - ry. Je - sus is a - live,

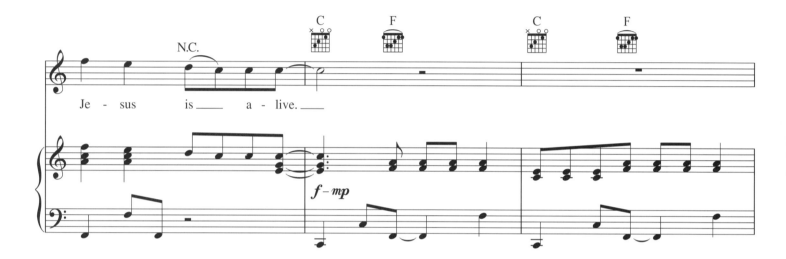

Je - sus is a - live.

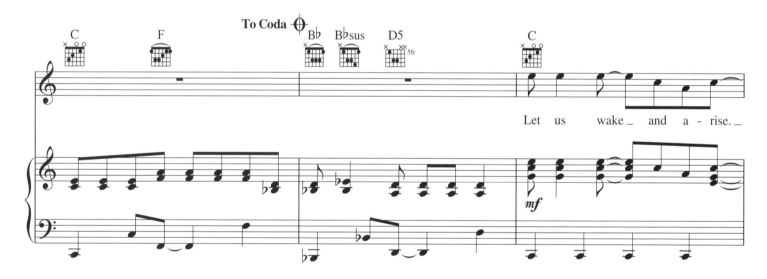

Let us wake and a - rise.

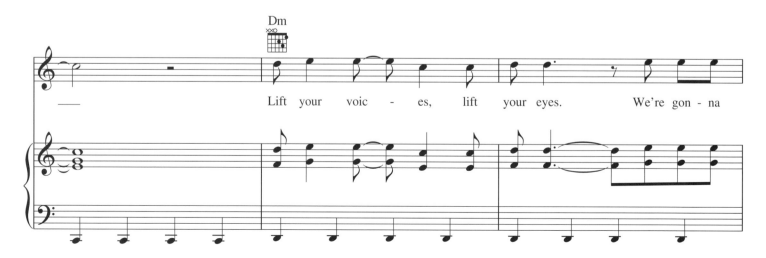

Lift your voic - es, lift your eyes. We're gon - na

shout, we're gon - na shake the ___ skies. ___ God is a - live. ___

We've been re - deemed, ___

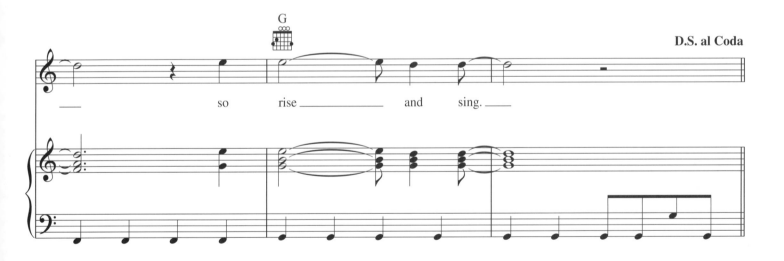

so rise ___ and sing. ___

D.S. al Coda

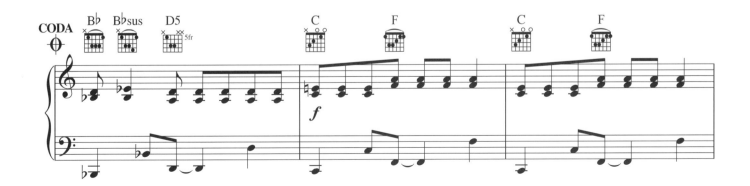

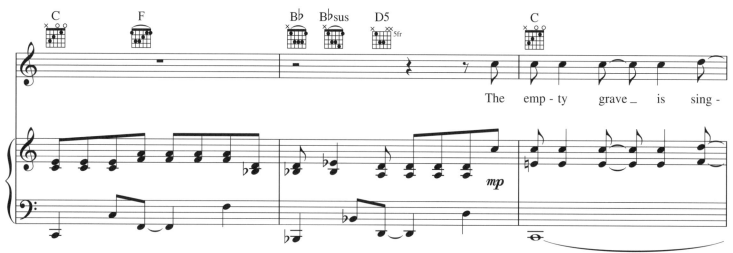

-ing out: ___ He is a-live, ___ He is a-live, ___

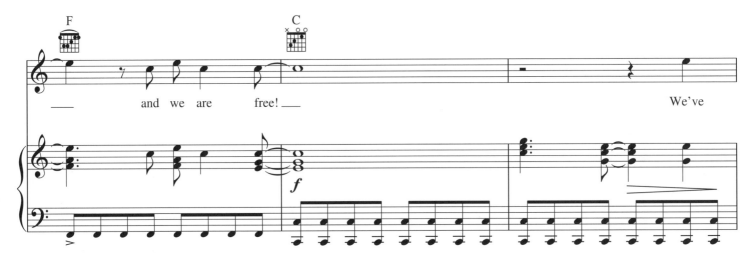

___ and we are free! ___ We've

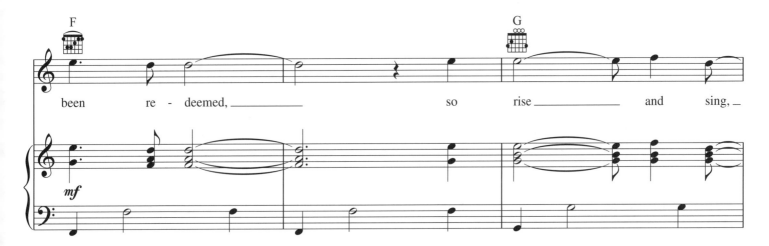

been re-deemed, ___ so rise ___ and sing, ___

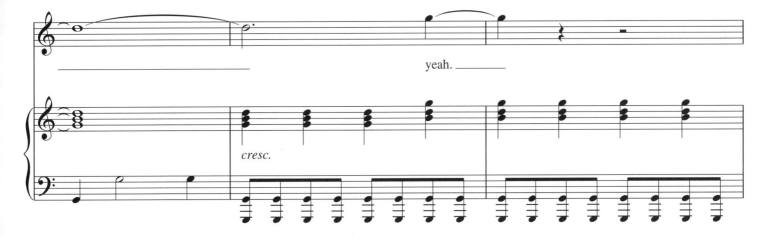

yeah. ___

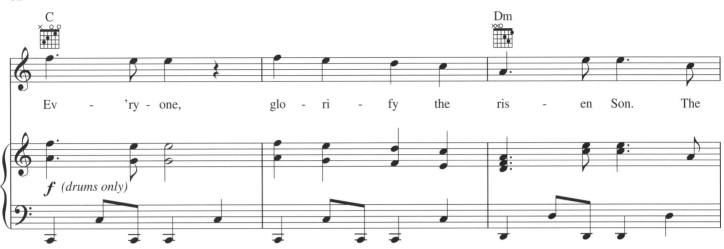

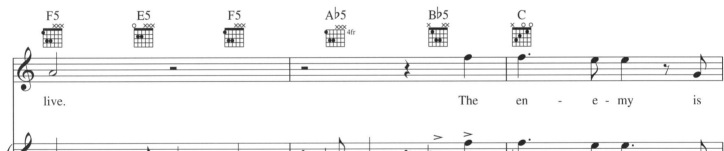

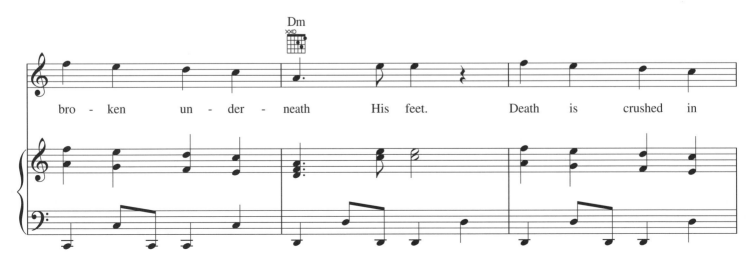

vic - to - ry.   Je - sus   is   a - live.

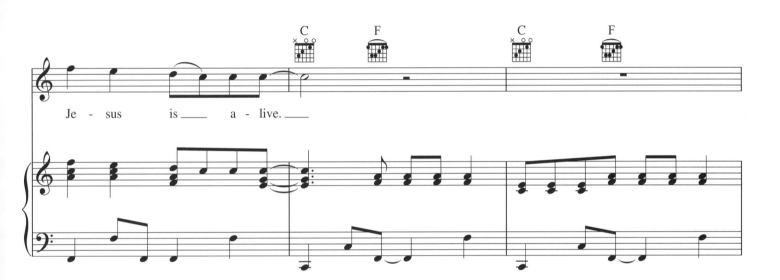

Je - sus   is____ a - live.____

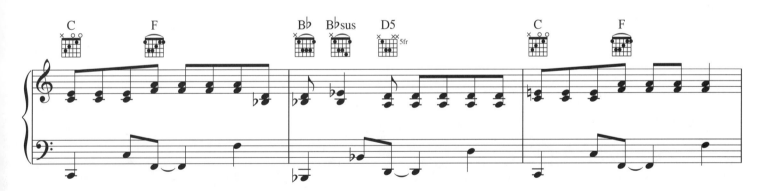

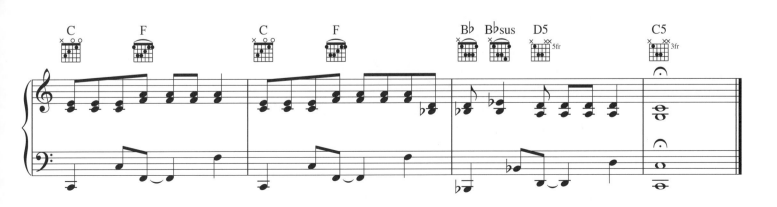

HE'S ALIVE

Words and Music by
DON FRANCISCO

Moderately, in 2

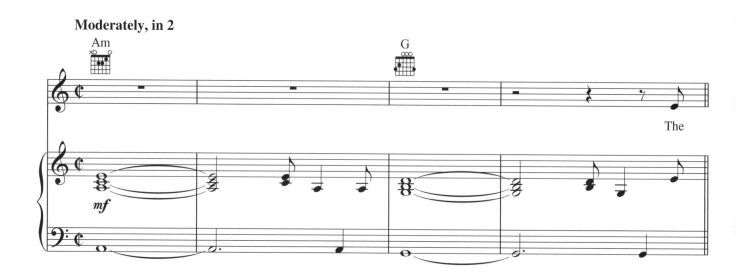

The

gates and doors were barred _____ and all the win-dows fas-tened down. I
just be-fore the sun — rise, _____ I heard some-thing at the wall. _____ The
no one there but Mar — y, _____ and so I went down to let her in. _____ The

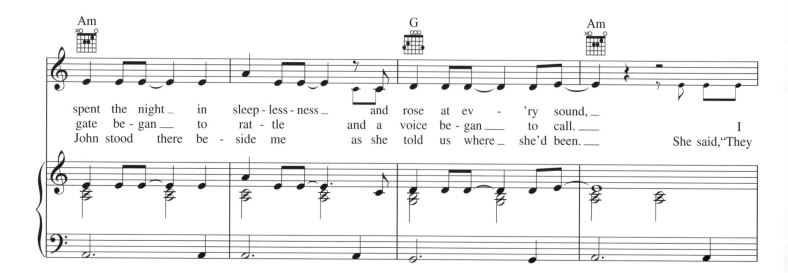

spent the night ___ in sleep-less-ness _____ and rose at ev-'ry sound, ___
gate be-gan ___ to rat - tle and a voice be-gan ___ to call. ___
John stood there be - side me as she told us where ___ she'd been. ___ She said,"They

I

emp - ty tomb just the way that Mar - y said. ___ But the wind - ing sheet they

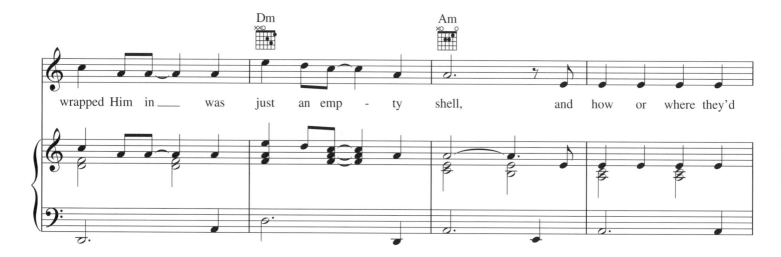

wrapped Him in ___ was just an emp - ty shell, ___ and how or where they'd

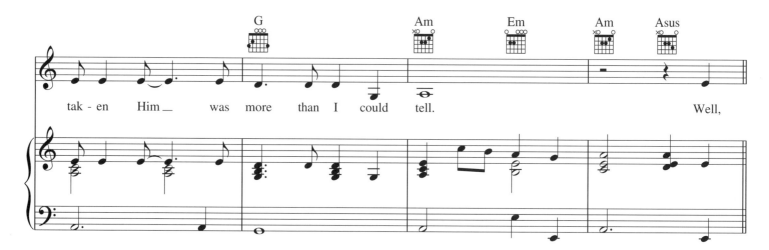

tak - en Him ___ was more than I could tell. ___ Well,

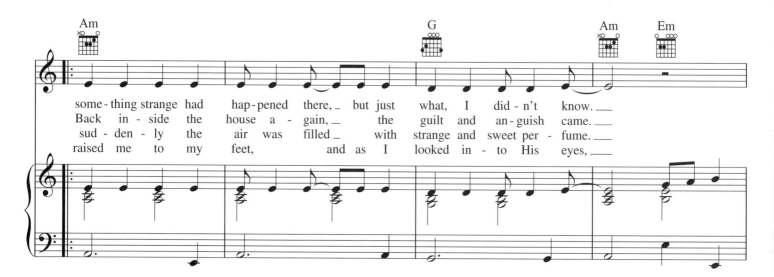

some - thing strange had hap - pened there, _ but just what, I did - n't know. ___
Back in - side the house a - gain, ___ the guilt and an - guish came. ___
sud - den - ly the air was filled _ with strange and sweet per - fume. ___
raised me to my feet, ___ and as I looked in - to His eyes, ___

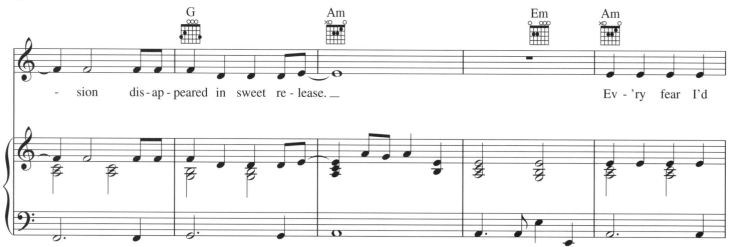

-sion dis-ap-peared in sweet re - lease. __ Ev - 'ry fear I'd

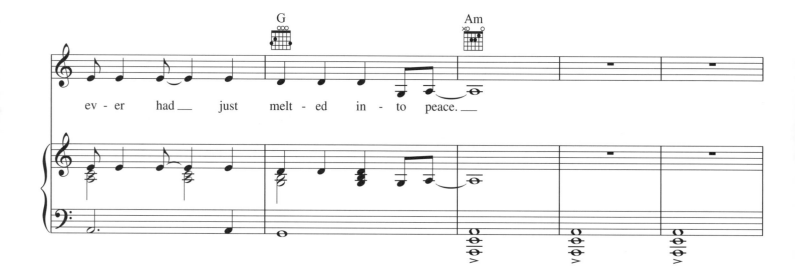

ev - er had __ just melt - ed in - to peace. __

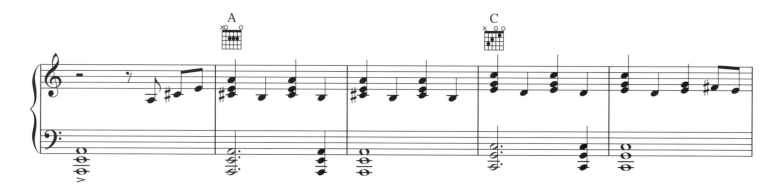

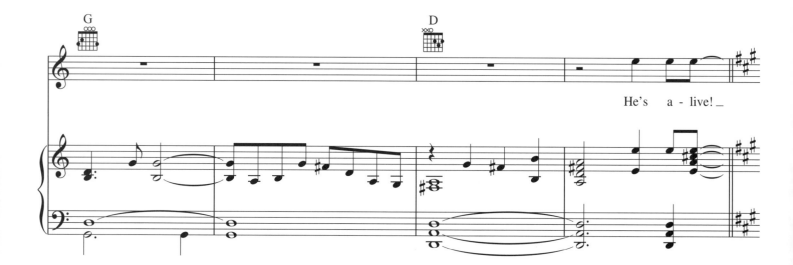

He's a - live! __

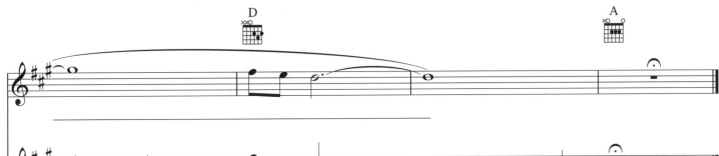

I'VE JUST SEEN JESUS

Words by GLORIA GAITHER
Music by WILLIAM J. GAITHER
and DANNY DANIELS

Slowly, with expression

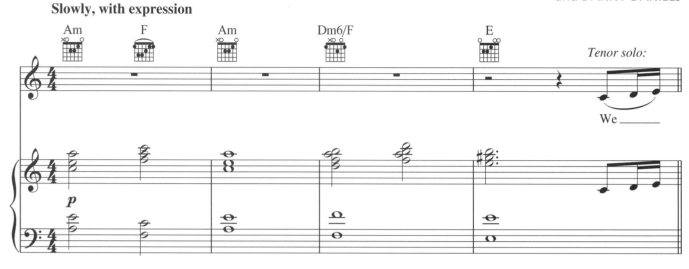

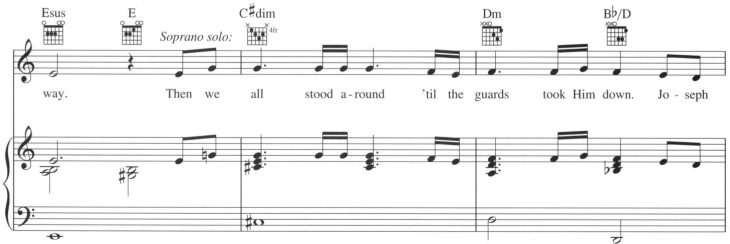

* Recorded a half step lower.

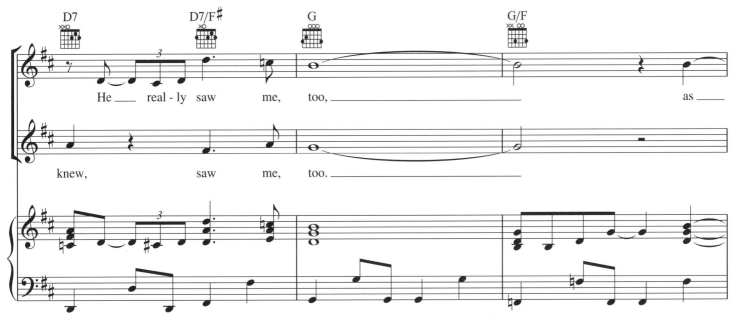

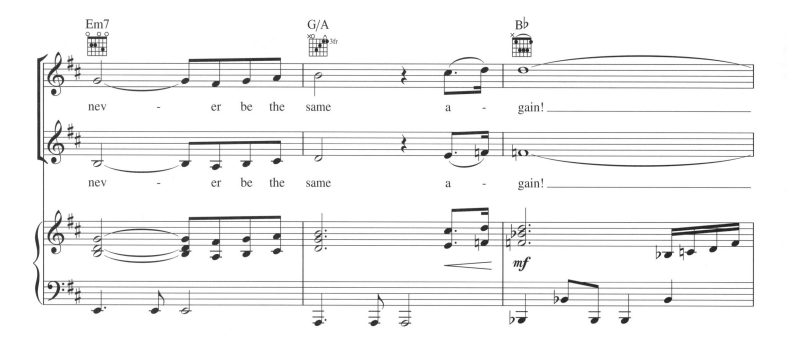

IN CHRIST ALONE

Words and Music by KEITH GETTY
and STUART TOWNEND

Moderately slow

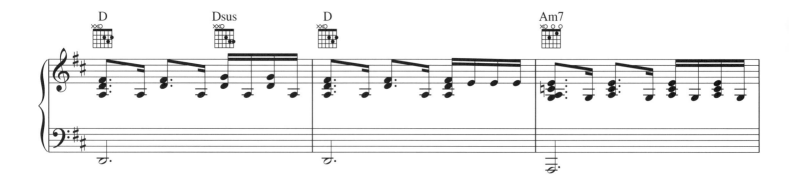

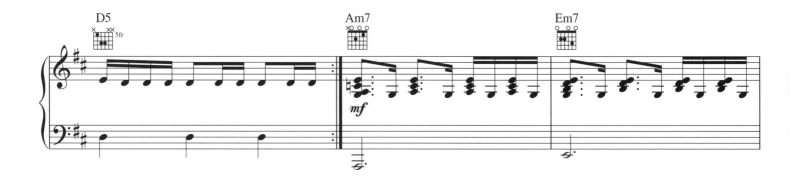

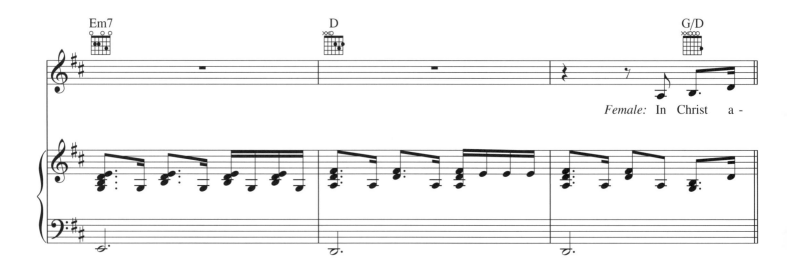

Female: In Christ a-

Asus A G D G A D/F♯
cease. My Com - fort - er, my All in All, here in the
fied, for ev - 'ry sin on Him was laid; here in the
G D/F♯ Em G/A
3fr
love of Christ I
death of Christ I
1
D G
stand. In Christ a -
2
D Am7 Em7
live. (Oh.
D Am7
Oh.)

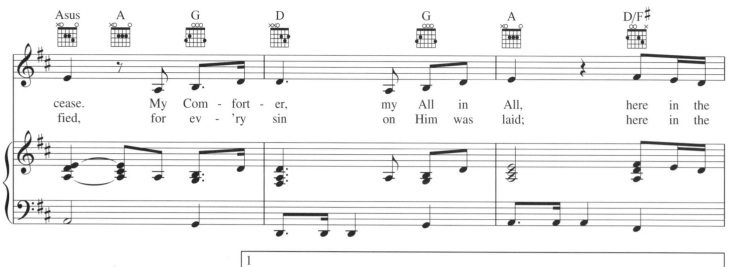

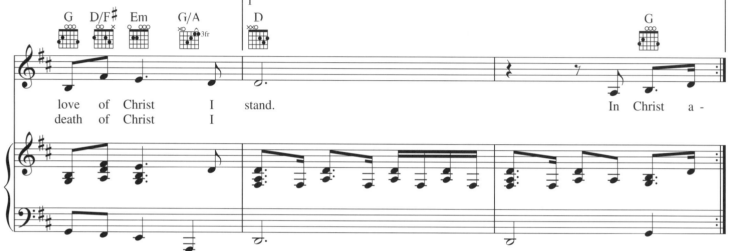

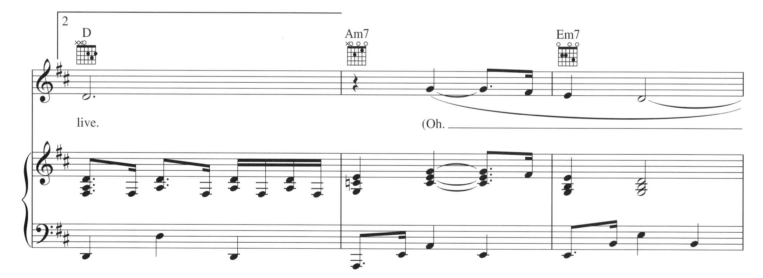

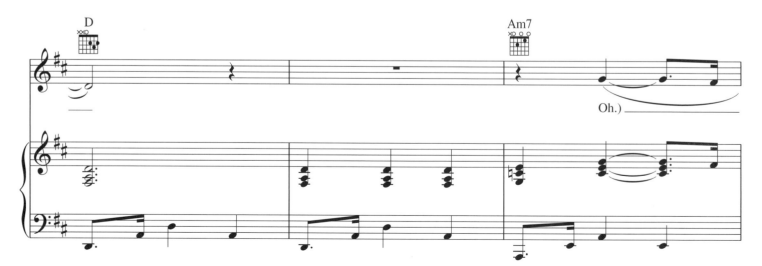

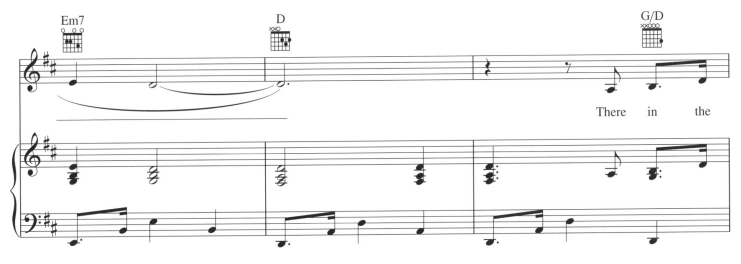

There in the

ground His bod-y lay, Light of the world by dark-ness slain. Then, burst-ing forth in glo-rious day, up from the

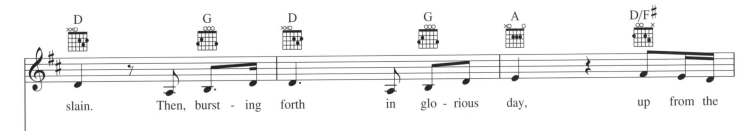

grave He rose a-gain! And as He stands in vic-to-

cresc.

f

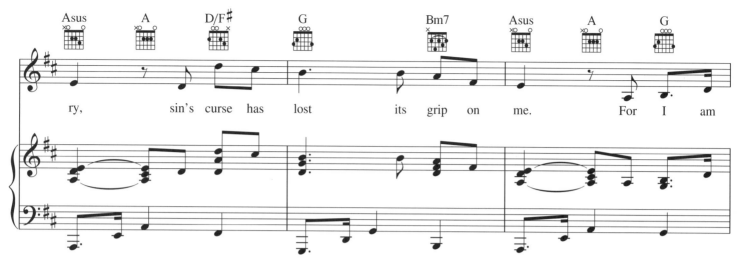

ry,   sin's curse has lost   its grip on me.   For I am

His   and He is mine,   bought with the pre - cious blood of

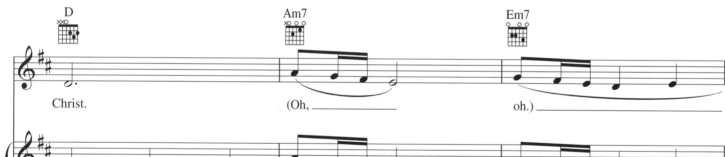

Christ.   (Oh, _____   oh.) _____

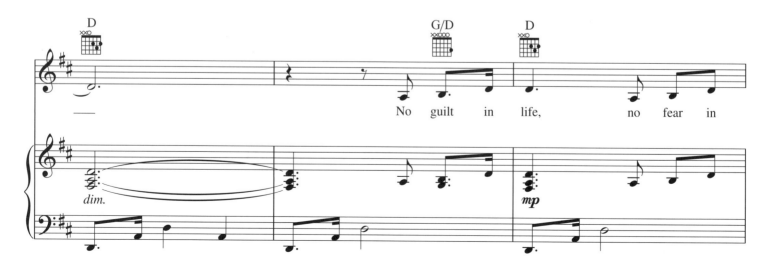

____   No guilt in life,   no fear in

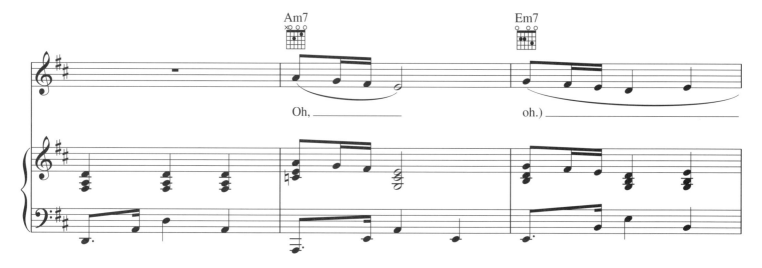

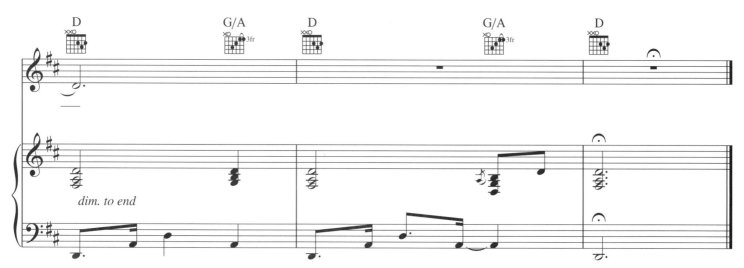

LOVE CRUCIFIED AROSE

Words and Music by
MICHAEL CARD

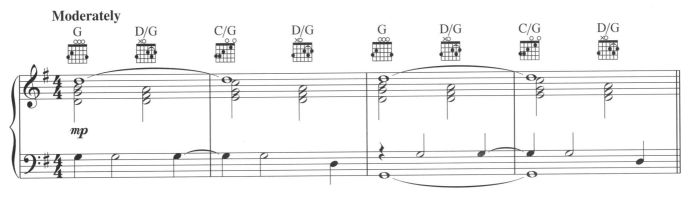

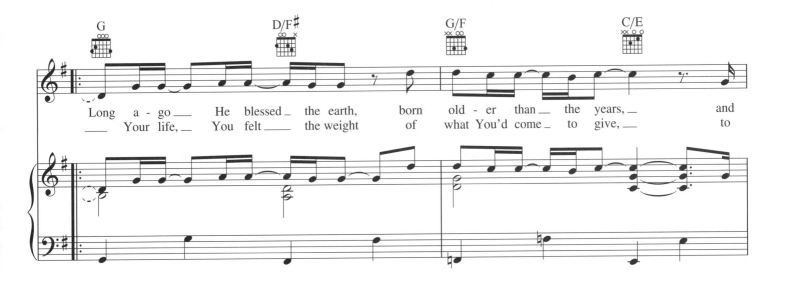

Long a - go __ He blessed __ the earth, born old - er than __ the years, __ and
__ Your life, __ You felt __ the weight of what You'd come __ to give, __ to

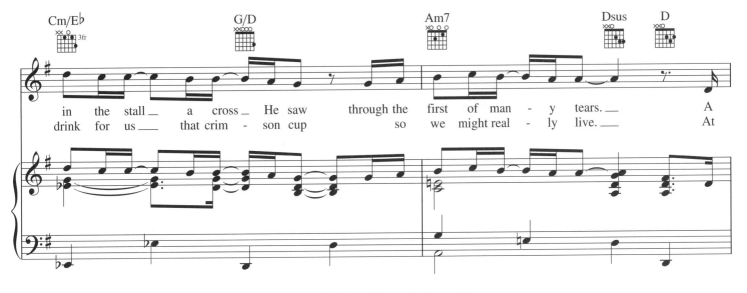

in the stall __ a cross __ He saw through the first of man - y tears. __ A
drink for us __ that crim - son cup so we might real - ly live. __ At

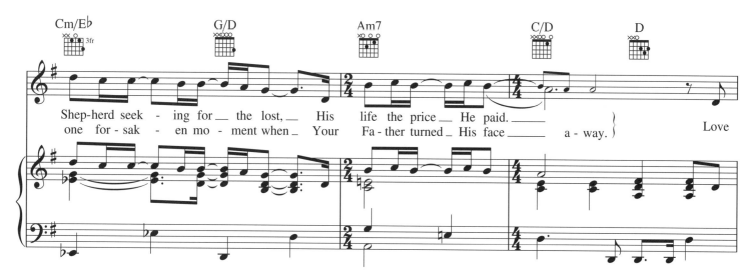

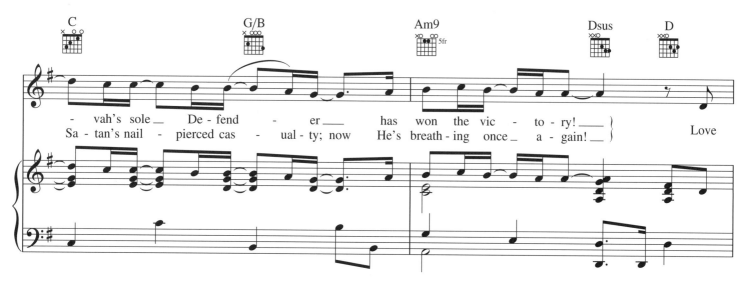

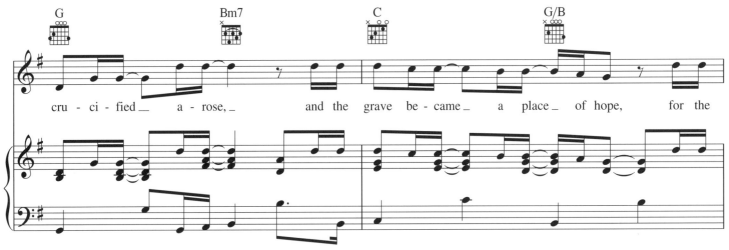

cru - ci - fied __ a - rose, __ and the grave be - came __ a place __ of hope, __ for the

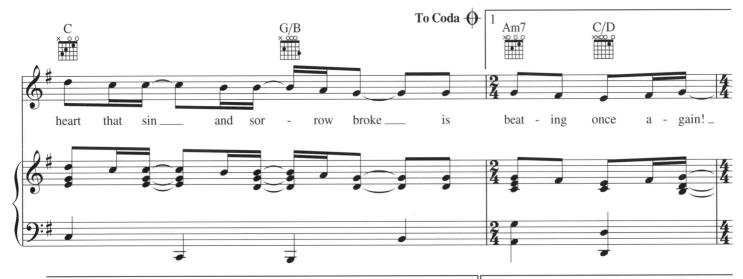

heart that sin __ and sor - row broke __ is beat - ing once a - gain! __

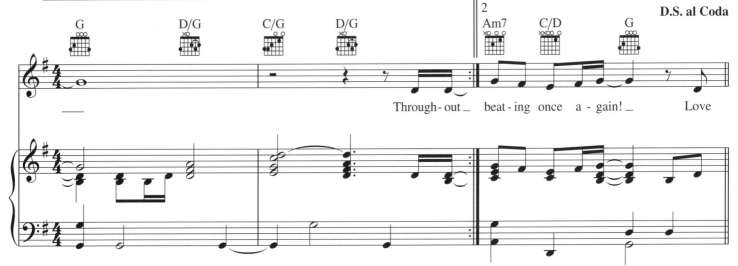

__ Through - out __ beat - ing once a - gain! __ Love

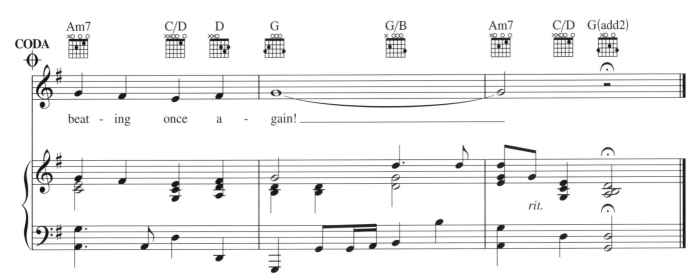

beat - ing once a - gain! _____

JESUS IS ALIVE

Words and Music by
RON KENOLY

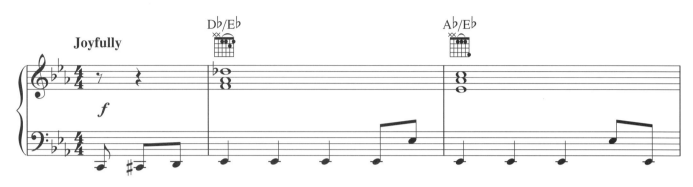

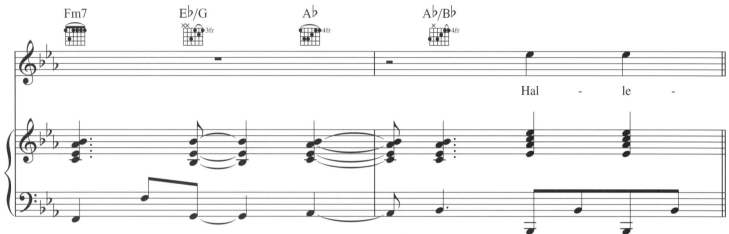

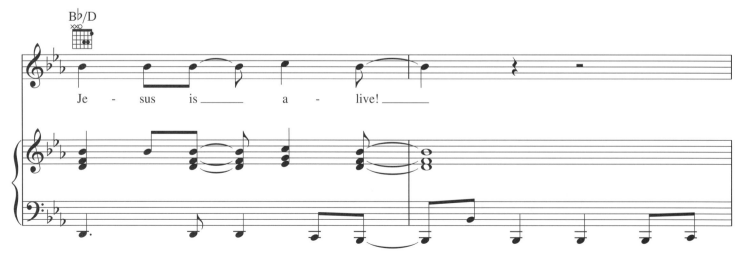

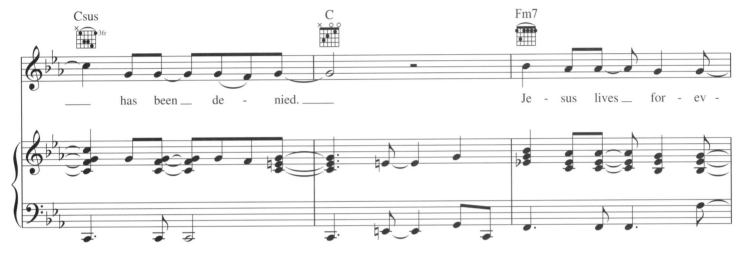

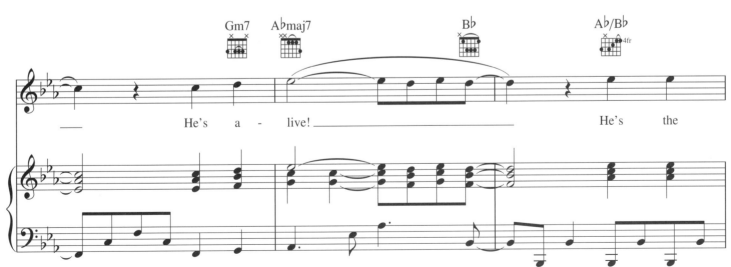

Al - pha and ___ O - me - ga, ___ the

First and Last ___ is He. ___ The curse of sin ___ is bro -

- ken and we have per - fect lib - er - ty. ___

___ The Lamb of God ___ has ris - en. He's a -

MIGHTY TO SAVE

Words and Music by BEN FIELDING
and REUBEN MORGAN

With praise

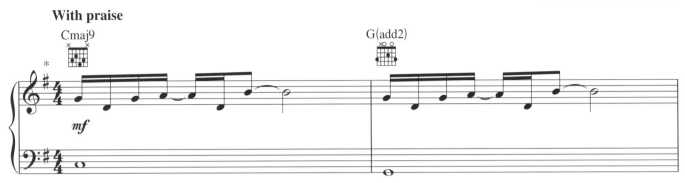

Ev-'ry-one needs com-pas - sion, a love that's nev-er-fail-

-ing. Let mer-cy fall on ___ me. Ev-'ry-one needs for-give-

* Recorded a half step lower.

- ness, the kind-ness of a Sav - ior, the hope of na - tions. —

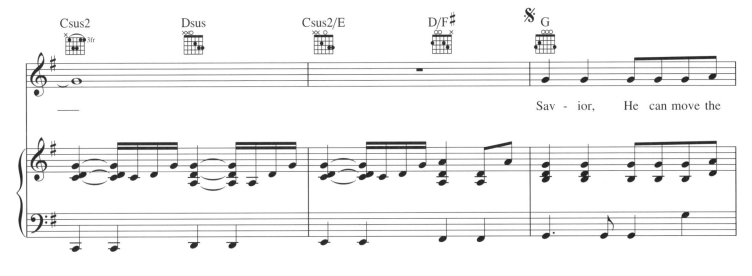

— Sav - ior, He can move the

moun - tains. My God is might-y to save, — He is might-y to save. — For -

ev - er Au - thor of sal - va - tion, He rose and con-quered the grave, — Je - sus

To Coda ⊕

con-quered the grave. _____

So take me as You find ___

___ me, all my fears and fail - ures; fill my life a - gain. ___

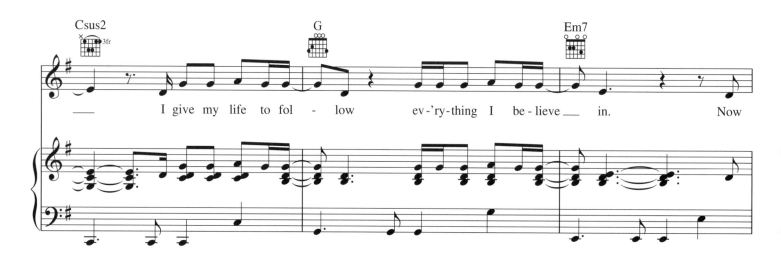

___ I give my life to fol - low ev - 'ry-thing I be - lieve ___ in. Now

D.S. al Coda

I sur - ren - der, _____ yes, I _____ sur - ren - der. _____

CODA

con - quered the grave. _____ Shine Your light and ___ let the whole world _

___ see we're sing-ing for the glo - ry ___ of the ris - en _____ King. _____ Je - sus,

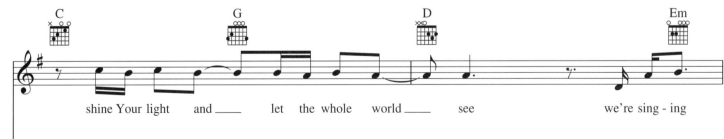

shine Your light and ___ let the whole world ___ see we're sing - ing

MY REDEEMER LIVES

Words and Music by
REUBEN MORGAN

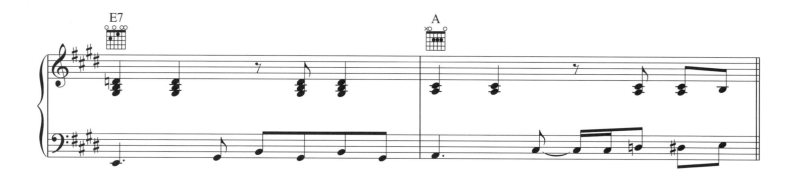

I know He res-cued my soul.

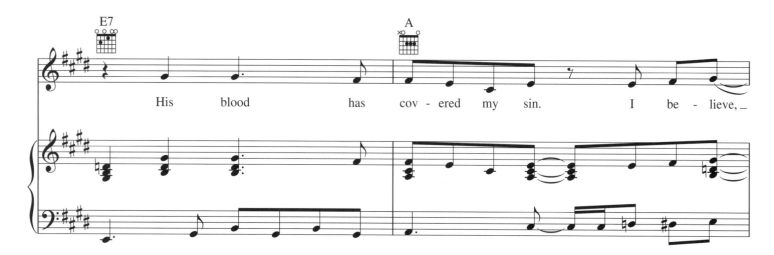

His blood has cov-ered my sin. I be-lieve,

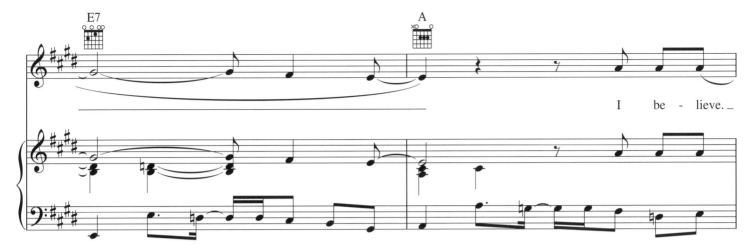

I be - lieve.

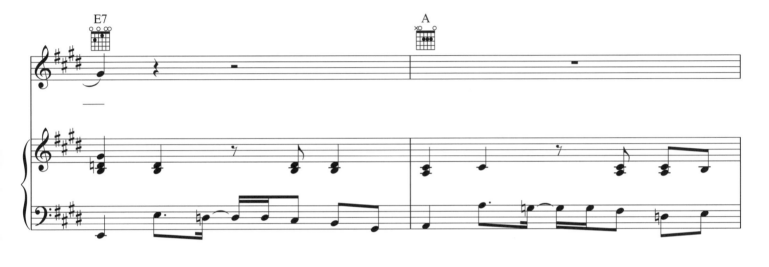

My shame He's tak - en a - way.

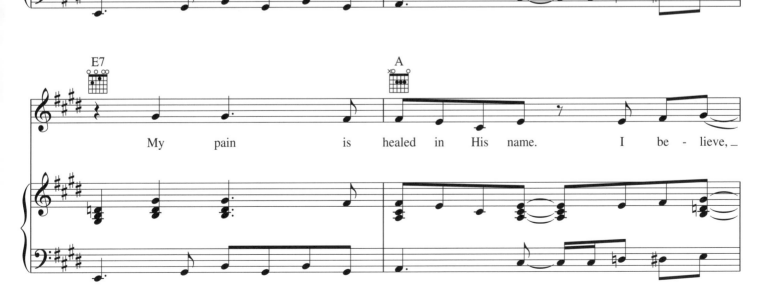

My pain is healed in His name. I be - lieve,

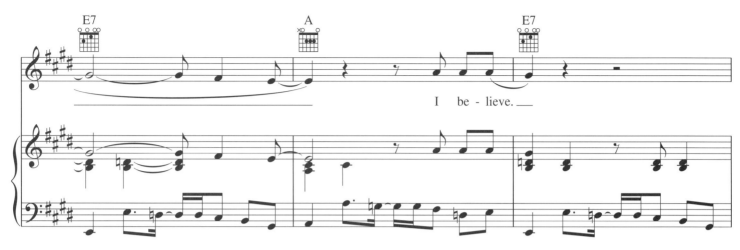

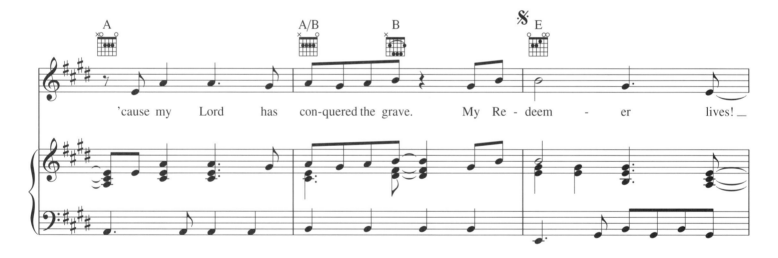

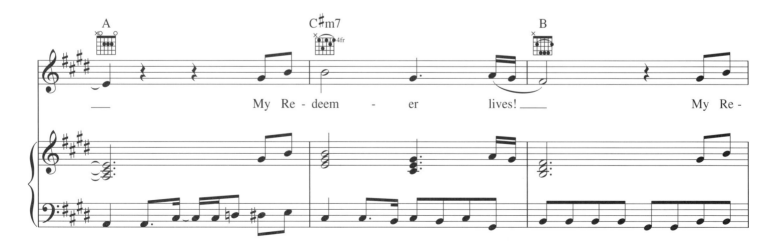

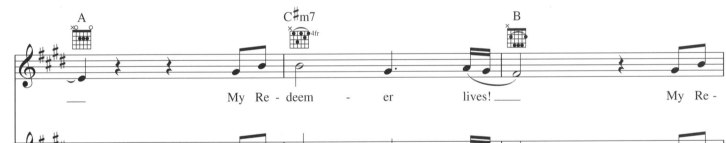

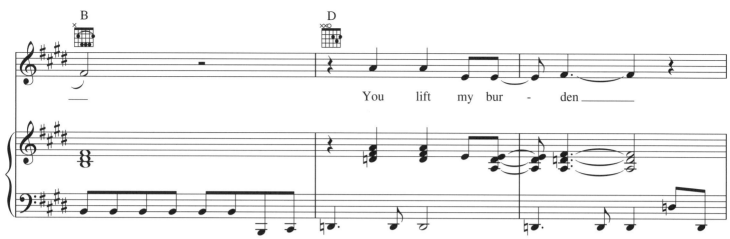

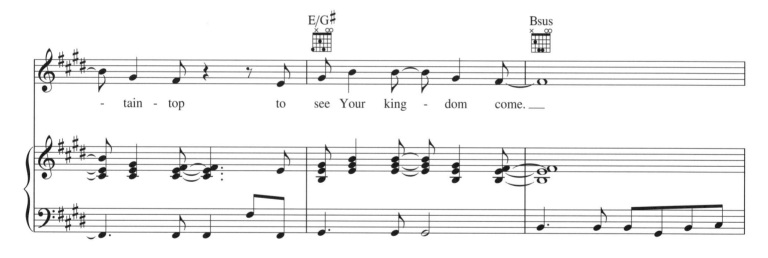

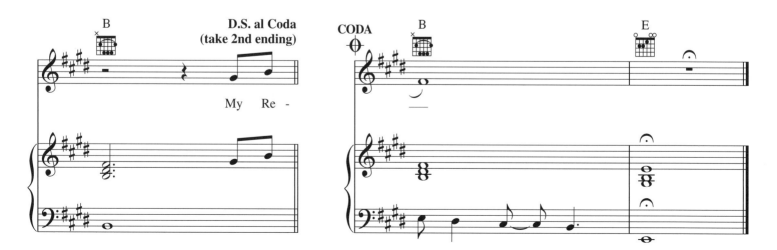

MY SAVIOR MY GOD

Words and Music by
AARON SHUST

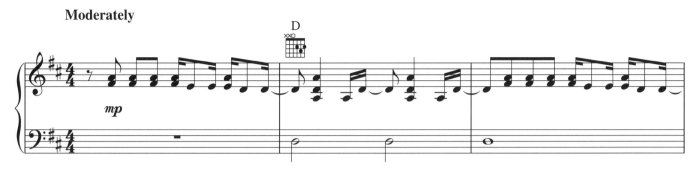

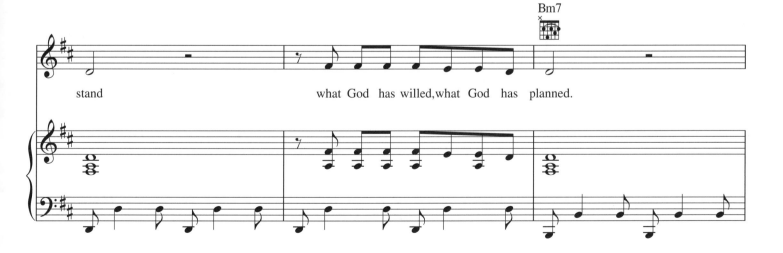

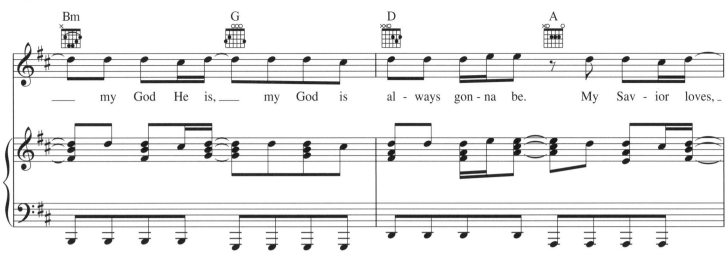

_____ my God He is, _____ my God is al - ways gon - na be. My Sav - ior loves, _____

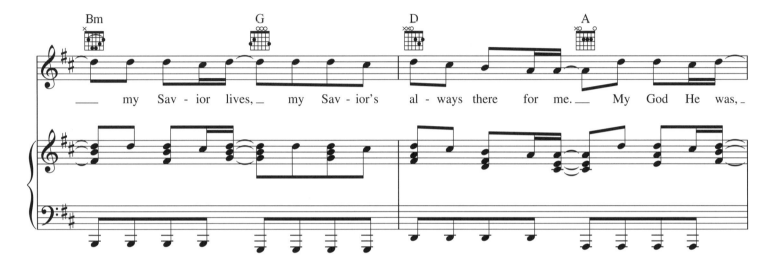

_____ my Sav - ior lives, _____ my Sav - ior's al - ways there for me. _____ My God He was, _____

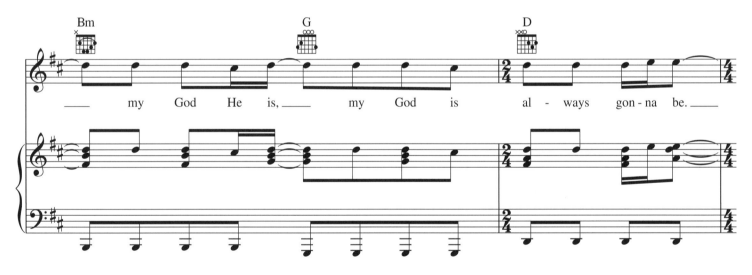

_____ my God He is, _____ my God is al - ways gon - na be. _____

_____

Yes, liv - ing, dy - ing, let me

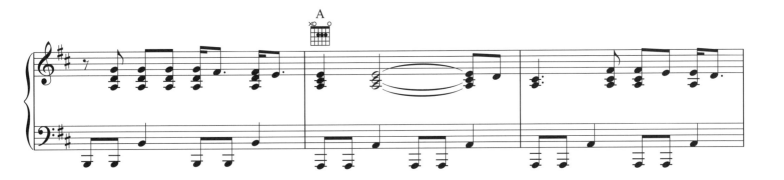

My Sav - ior loves, ___ my Sav - ior lives, ___ my Sav - ior's

al - ways there for me. ___ My God He was, ___ my God He is, ___ my God is

al - ways gon - na be. My Sav - ior loves, __ my Sav - ior lives, __ my Sav - ior's

al - ways there for me. __ My God He was, __ my God He is, __ my God is

al - ways gon - na be. My Sav - ior loves, __ my Sav - ior lives, __ my Sav - ior's

al - ways there for me. __ My God He was, __ my God He is, __ my God is

al - ways gon - na be. My Sav - ior loves, ___ my Sav - ior lives, _ my Sav - ior's

al - ways there for me. __ My God He was, ___ my God He is, __ my God is

al - ways gon - na be. My Sav - ior lives, __ my Sav - ior loves, _ my Sav - ior lives, _

dim. to end

__ my Sav - ior loves, __ my Sav - ior lives. __

MY SAVIOR LIVES

Words and Music by JON EGAN
and GLENN PACKIAM

Recorded a half step lower.

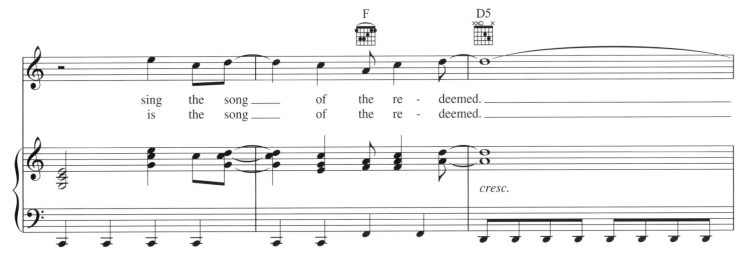

sing the song ____ of the re - deemed. _____
is the song ____ of the re - deemed. _____

cresc.

____ I know that my ____ Re - deem - er lives,

f

and now I stand ____ on what ____ He did. My Sav - ior,

my Sav - ior lives. ____

Ev - 'ry day a brand - new chance __ to say, "Je - sus, You are __

__ the on - ly way." My Sav - ior, my Sav - ior lives. __

My Sav - ior _____ lives, _____ yeah.

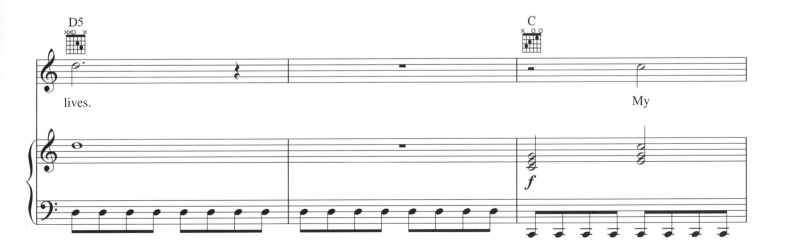

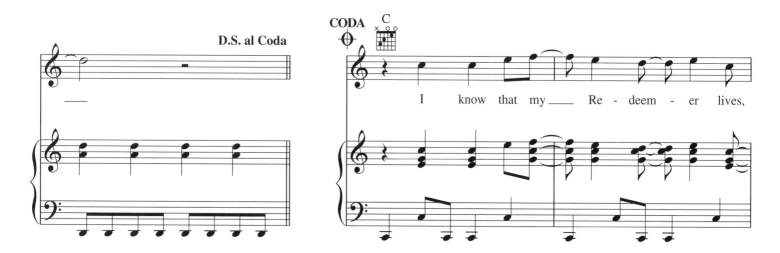

my Sav - ior _____ lives. _____

My Sav - ior, my Sav - ior _____ lives.

My Sav - ior, my Sav - ior lives.

REDEEMER

Words and Music by
NICOLE C. MULLEN

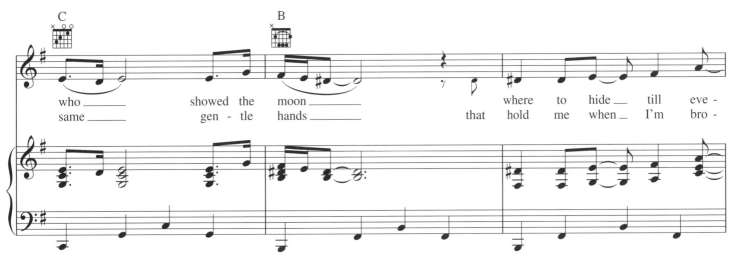

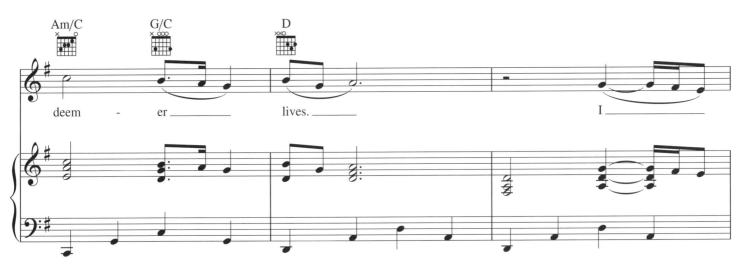

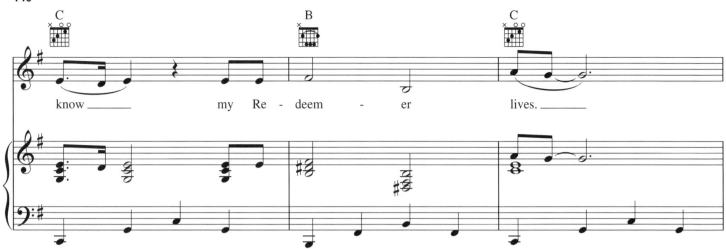

know _____ my Re - deem - er lives. _____

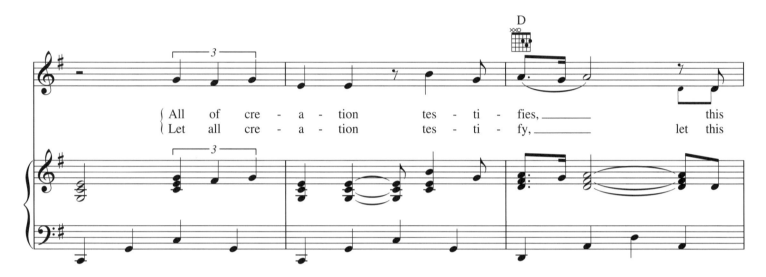

All of cre - a - tion tes - ti - fies, _____ this
Let all cre - a - tion tes - ti - fy, _____ let this

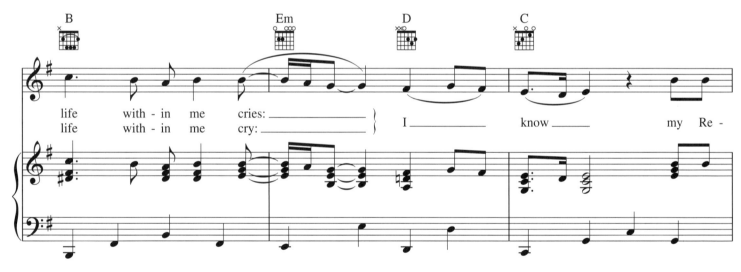

life with - in me cries: _____
life with - in me cry: _____
I _____ know _____ my Re -

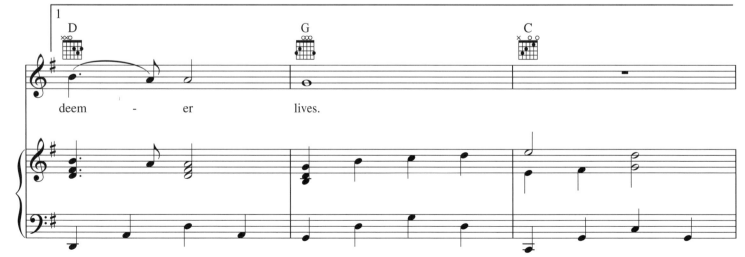

deem - er lives.

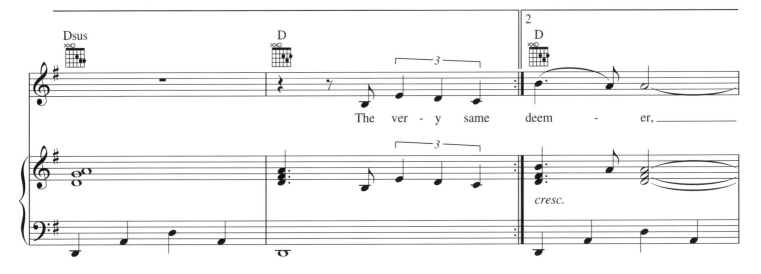

The ver - y same deem - er, _____

He lives to take a - way my

shame. _____ And He _____ lives; for -

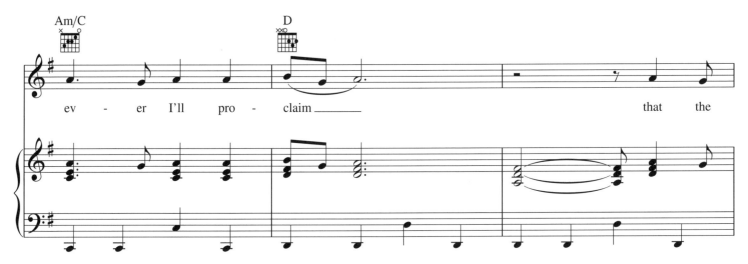

ev - er I'll pro - claim _____ that the

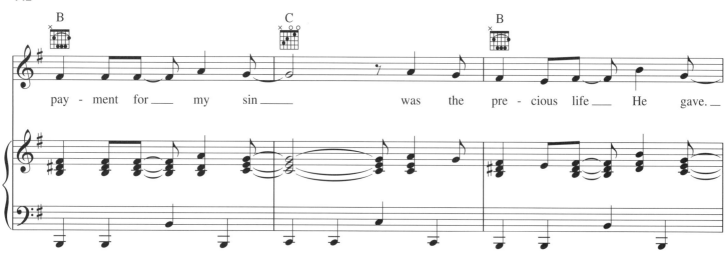

deem - er lives. _____ Let all cre -

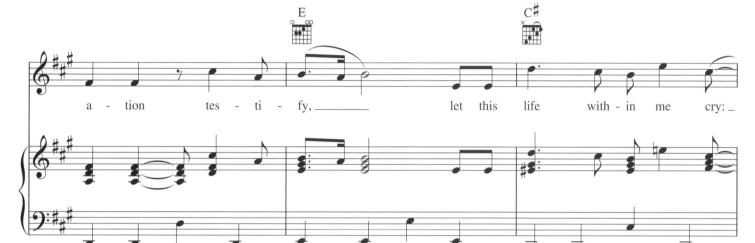

a - tion tes - ti - fy, _____ let this life with - in me cry: _

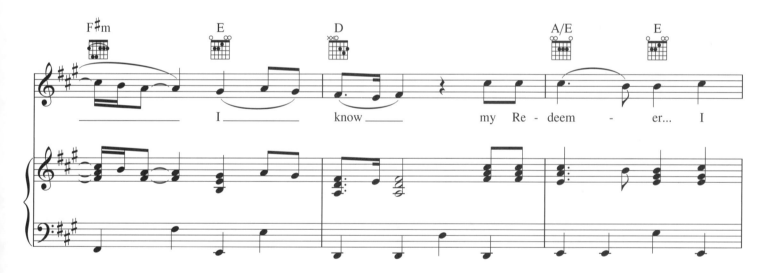

_____ I _____ know _____ my Re - deem - er... I

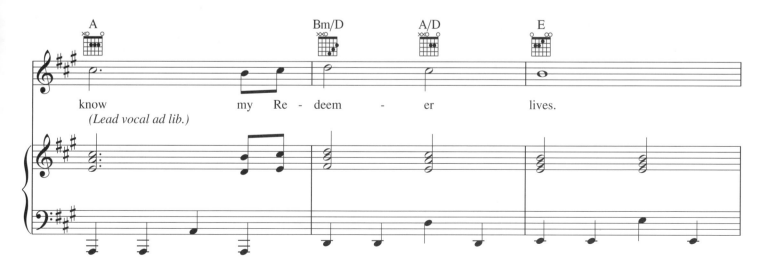

know my Re - deem - er lives.
(Lead vocal ad lib.)

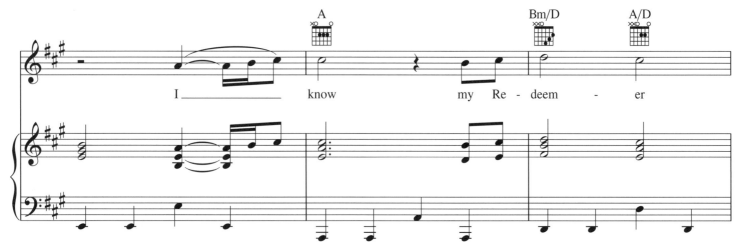

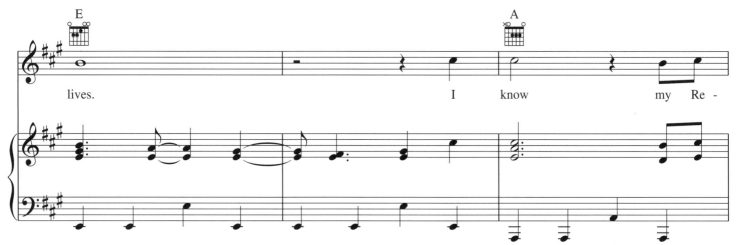

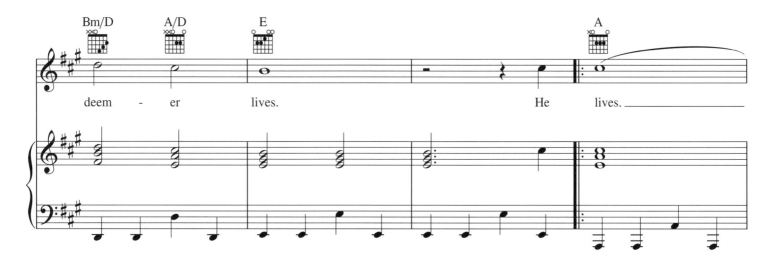

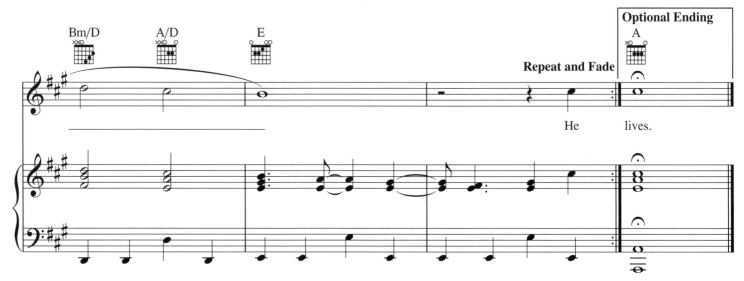

STRONGER

Words and Music by BEN FIELDING
and REUBEN MORGAN

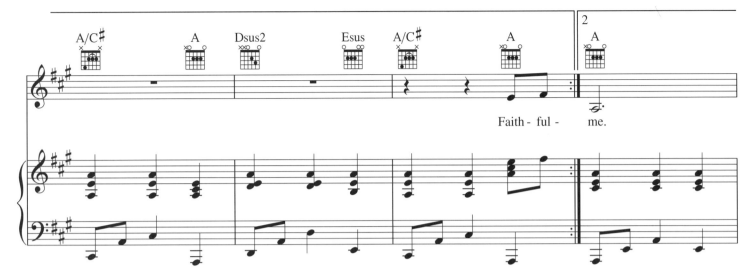

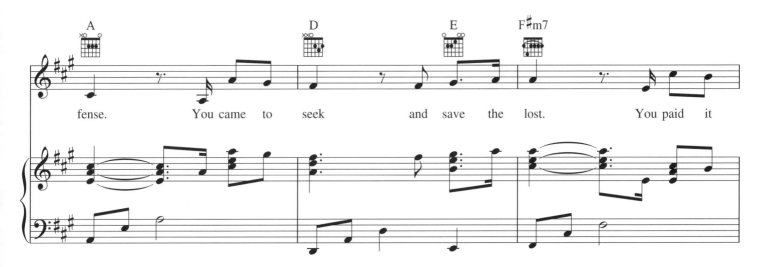

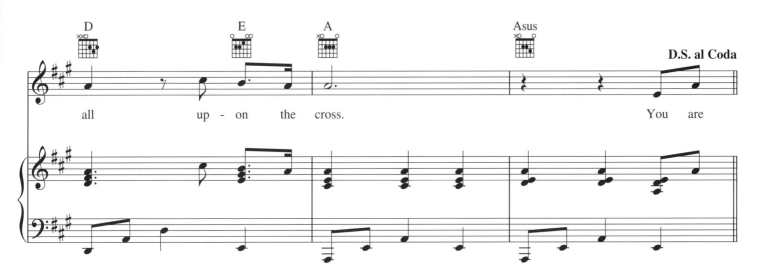

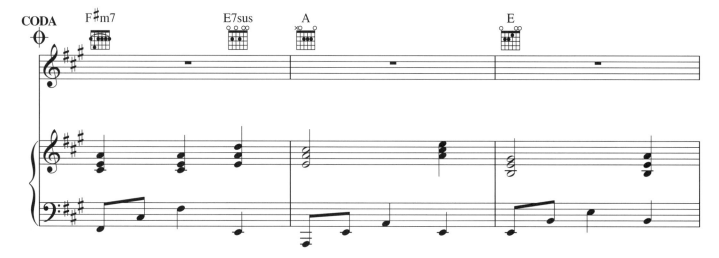

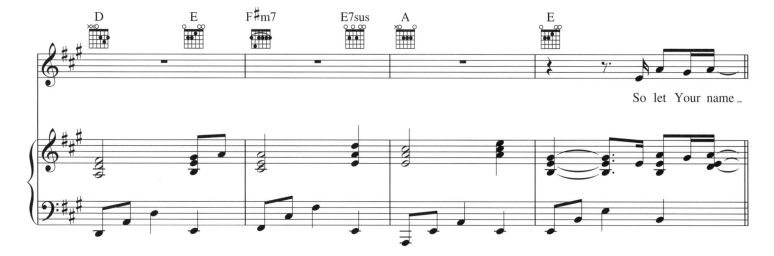

So let Your name __

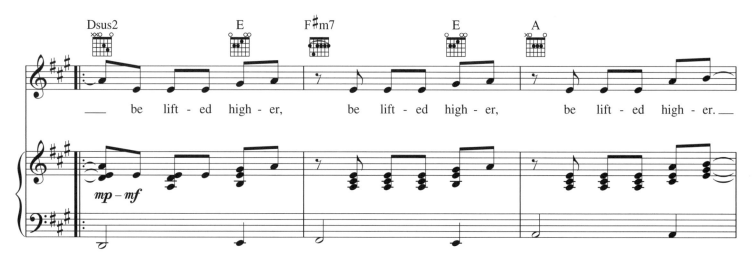

__ be lift - ed high - er, be lift - ed high - er, be lift - ed high - er. __

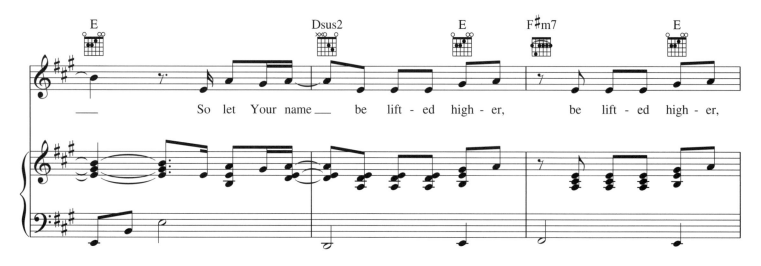

__ So let Your name __ be lift - ed high - er, be lift - ed high - er,

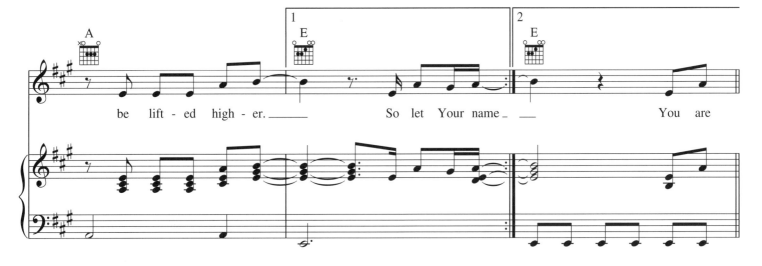

be lift - ed high - er._____ So let Your name____ You are

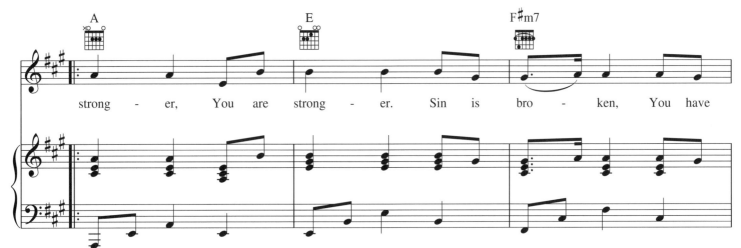

strong - er, You are strong - er. Sin is bro - ken, You have

saved me. It is writ - ten: Christ is ris - en. Je - sus,

You are Lord of all. You are all.

SAVED THE DAY

Words and Music by
MICHAEL NEALE

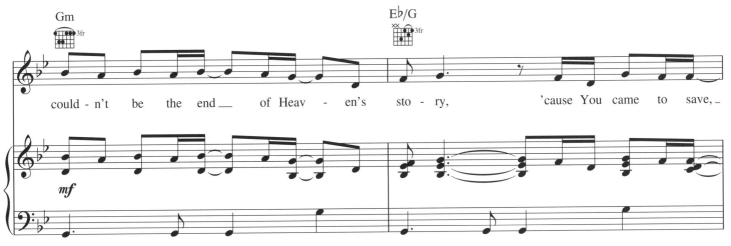

the day You rolled ___ the stone ___ a - way. ___ The emp - ty grave ___

___ is there ___ to say, ___ "You reign!" ___ You saved the day. ___

___ You tore the ho - ly veil ___ a - way, ___ You o - pened wide ___

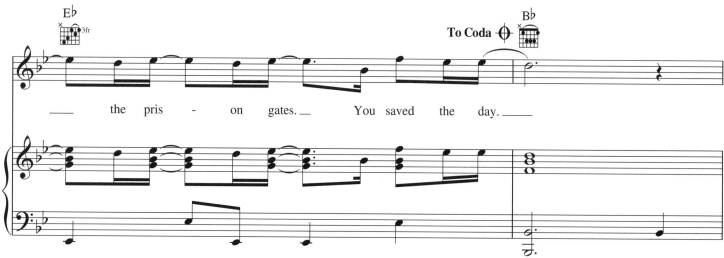

___ the pris - on gates. ___ You saved the day. ___

Oh God,__ You res - cued me __

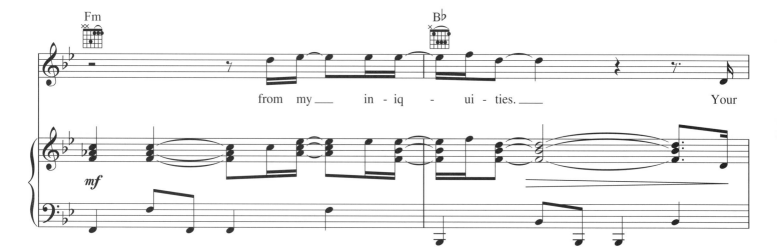

from my __ in - iq - ui - ties. __ Your

gift of love __ is hope __ that springs _ e - ter - nal. And be - cause of You __

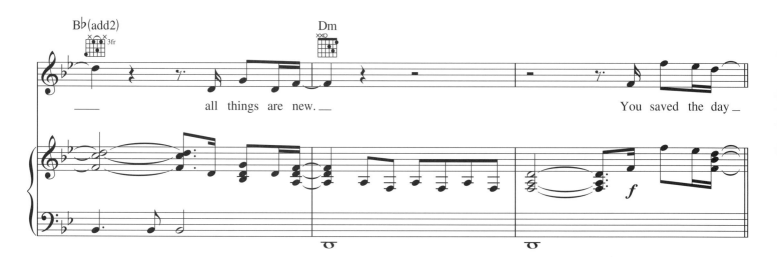

__ all things are new. __ You saved the day __

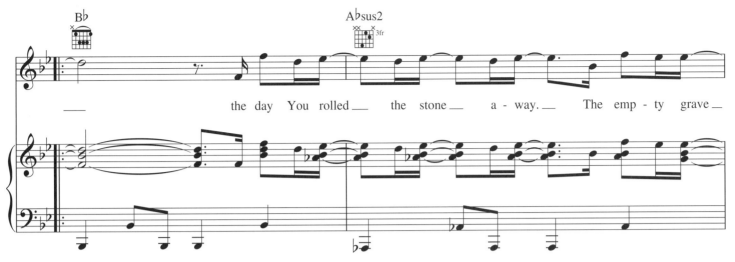

the day You rolled __ the stone __ a - way. __ The emp - ty grave __

__ is there __ to say, __ "You reign!" __ You saved the day. __

__ You tore the ho - ly veil __ a - way, __ You o - pened wide __

__ the pris - on gates. __ You saved the day. _____ You saved the day __ __

WAS IT A MORNING LIKE THIS?

Words and Music by
JIM CROEGAERT

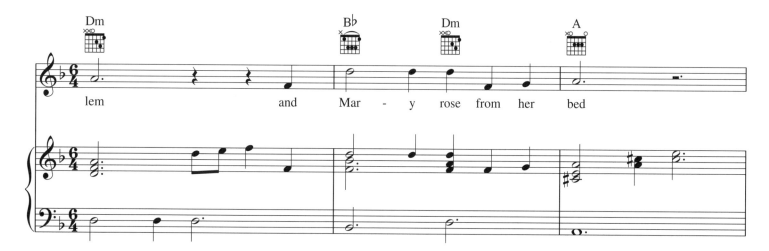

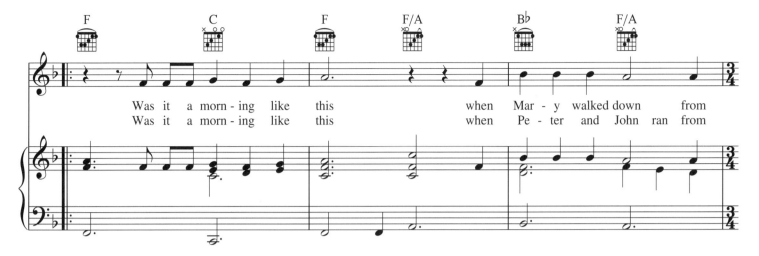

Was it a morn-ing like this when Mar - y walked down from
Was it a morn-ing like this when Pe - ter and John ran from

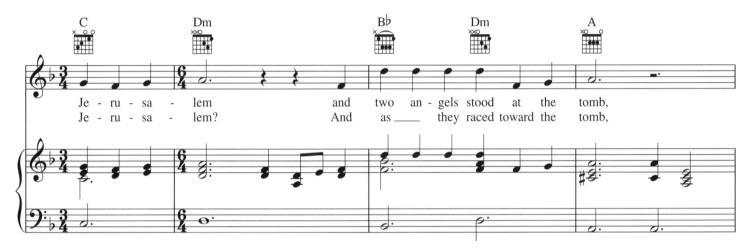

Je - ru - sa - lem and two an - gels stood at the tomb,
Je - ru - sa - lem? And as ___ they raced toward the tomb,

bear - ers of news she would hear soon? ___ Did the
be - neath their feet was there a tune? ___

grass sing? Did the earth re - joice to feel You a - gain? ___

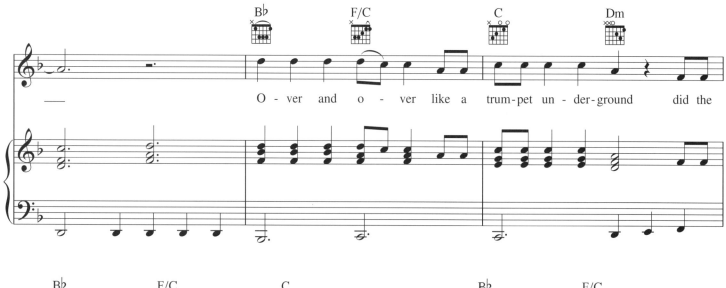

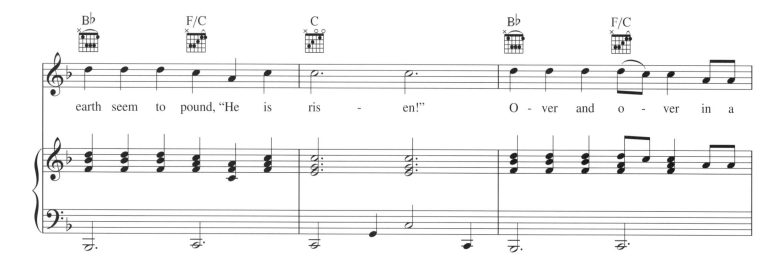

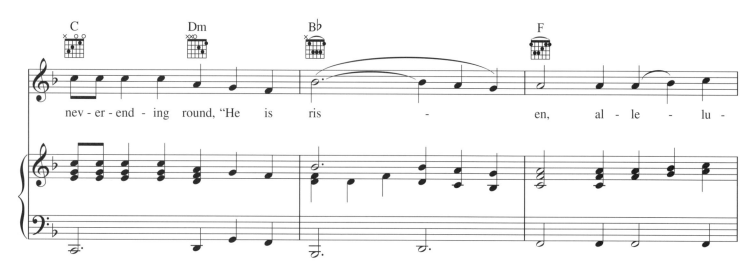

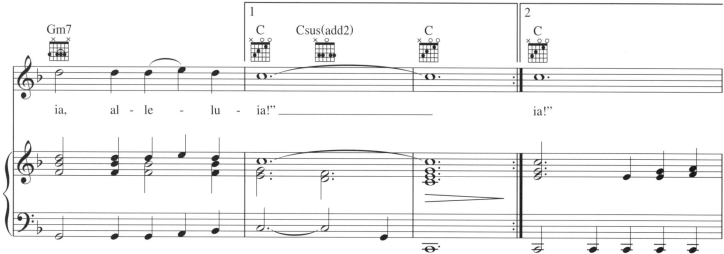

O - ver and o - ver like a trum-pet un - der-ground did the earth seem to pound, "He is

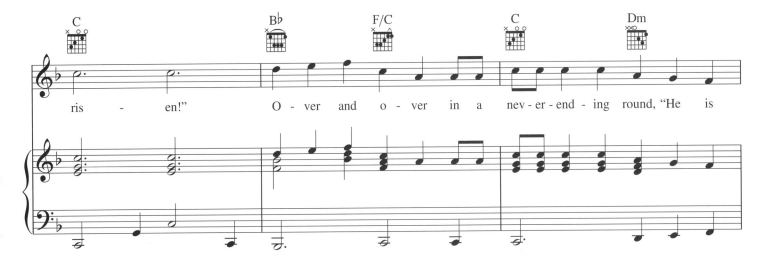

ris - en!" O - ver and o - ver in a nev-er-end - ing round, "He is

ris - en, al - le - lu - ia, al - le - lu -

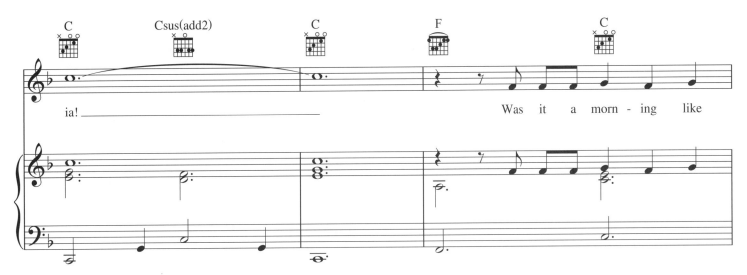

ia! _____ Was it a morn - ing like

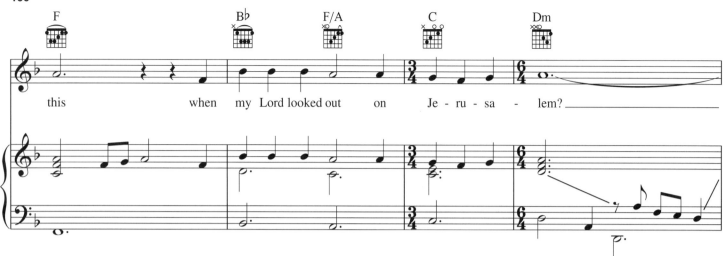

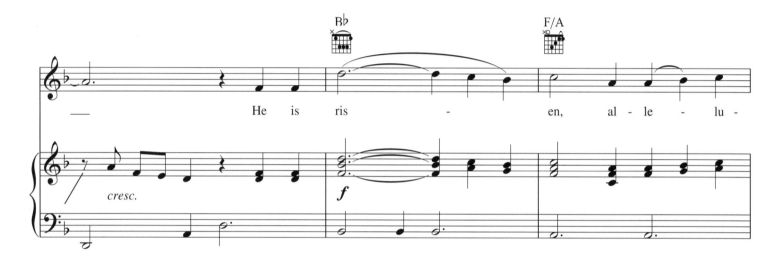

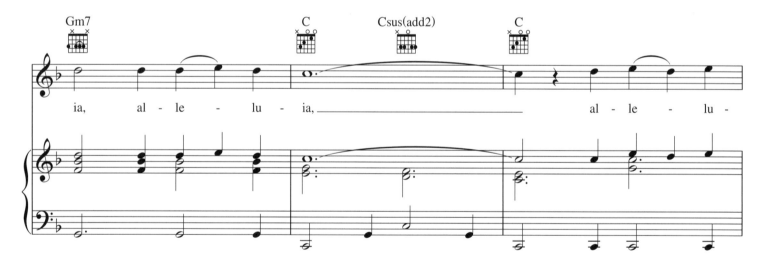

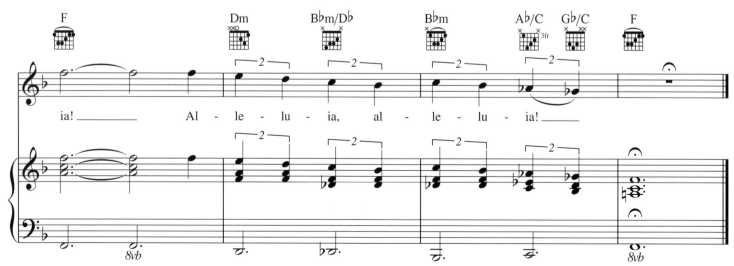